The Weight of Things

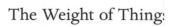

For my parents,

for Peter,

and for Becky and Sammy

The Weight of Things

Philosophy and the Good Life

Jean Kazez

Blackwell
Publishing

"Closer to Fine": words and music by Emily Saliers © 1989
EMI VIRGIN SONGS, INC. and GODHAP MUSIC. All rights controlled and
administered by EMI VIRGIN SONGS, INC. All rights reserved. International
copyright secured. Used by permission.

BLACKWELL PUBLISHING
350 Main Street, Malden, MA 02148-5020, USA
9600 Garsington Road, Oxford OX4 2DQ, UK
550 Swanston Street, Carlton, Victoria 3053, Australia

First published 2007 by Blackwell Publishing Ltd

1   2007

Library of Congress Cataloging-in-Publication Data

Kazez, Jean.
  The weight of things : philosophy and the good life / Jean Kazez.
    p. cm.
  Includes bibliographical references (p.) and index.
  ISBN-13: 978-1-4051-6077-3 (hardcover : alk. paper)
  ISBN-13: 978-1-4051-6078-0 (pbk. : alk. paper)
  1. Life. 2. Conduct of life. 3. Ethics. 4. Happiness. 5. Values.
I. Title.

BD431.K39 2007
170—dc22

                                                    2006027960

A catalogue record for this title is available from the British Library.

Set in 11/13.5pt Dante
by SNP Best-set Typesetters Ltd, Hong Kong
Printed and bound in Singapore
by C.O.S. Printers Pte Ltd

The publisher's policy is to use permanent paper from mills that operate a
sustainable forestry policy, and which has been manufactured from pulp
processed using acid-free and elementary chlorine-free practices. Furthermore,
the publisher ensures that the text paper and cover board used have met
acceptable environmental accreditation standards.

For further information on
Blackwell Publishing, visit our website:
www.blackwellpublishing.com

Will not the knowledge of [the good], then, have a great influence on life? Shall we not, like archers who have a mark to aim at, be more likely to hit upon what we should? If so, we must try, in outline at least, to determine what it is . . .

Aristotle, *Nicomachean Ethics*, Book I, Chapter 2

I went to the doctor, I went to the mountains
I looked to the children, I drank from the fountains
there's more than one answer to these questions
pointing me in a crooked line
and the less I seek my source for some definitive
the closer I am to fine
the closer I am to fine

Emily Saliers, "Closer to Fine"

Contents

Introduction

It's not every day that we examine our lives. Some of our happiest moments take place when we are least in the mood for examining anything. You look at your child, the view from a mountaintop, your new car, or whatever it is you most enjoy, and you think – I want nothing more than this. Or you don't think at all; you just enjoy.

Reflection can begin for many reasons. On major birthdays we can wonder whether we are moving in the right direction. A brush with a serious illness is often a time of reflection about what really matters and what doesn't. At the end of life, you may find yourself asking whether you got to have the life you wanted.

Sometimes it's other people that get us thinking. After reading about customs in another culture, we might wonder whether our lives are missing something, or theirs are misguided. A friend's life takes some strange turn and we begin to think about our priorities – and our friend's.

All of these situations drive us toward *philosophy*: toward questions of value, of what is better or worse, of the way we *ought* to live. They have been dealt with by ethicists since ancient times, though in some periods more directly than in others. For Plato and Aristotle and all the ancient schools that came after them, the question about how we should live is a question about the "highest good," the ultimate thing I ought to aim for. The nineteenth century was another period of direct and intense focus on questions about life as a whole. "Good" is too bland a word for the life Nietzsche admires – he urges his readers to "live dangerously." "Build your cities on the slopes of Vesuvius!" he writes. The existentialists of the twentieth century were also in the business of addressing the question of how to live, but the flavor is again something new. It may not be possible to live a life that is simply good, they suggest, but we can live with a more honest acceptance of the human condition.

Philosophers today still address the most fundamental questions about how we should live. Is happiness the only thing that matters? Robert Nozick says "no," making an argument that is a model of the way argumentation can be brought to bear on these "big" issues (turn to Chapter 4 quickly, if you're skeptical of the possibility of having rational debates about values). What else *could* you place at the core of living well? Two contemporary views that demand to be taken seriously are Peter Singer's and Martha Nussbaum's. In *How Are We to Live?* Singer argues that living well means living with a focus beyond oneself. Strongly influenced by Aristotelian ideas, Martha Nussbaum stresses the realization of basic human capabilities in *Women and Human Development*.

Despite the historic and contemporary philosophical interest in the good life, today people wanting to think about life issues will likely head to the religion or psychology or self-help sections of the bookstore. This is partly the fault of philosophers themselves. Rare is the book of philosophy that's designed to be enjoyed. The three authors I've mentioned are good writers, but only Singer aims for general accessibility.

The problem with consigning the topic of living to psychologists and religious writers is that they don't ask the questions philosophers do. Is living well bound up with religion? The books from the religion shelves assume one thing, without taking alternatives seriously. Most of the books from the psychology section assume a secular answer, without taking the religious answer seriously. Is there really any right way to live, instead of different right ways for different people? That's a question that an "advice" or "how to" book won't broach. Is there one thing that ought to be everybody's aim? It might be inspirational to read a book that says so, but there are arguments on both sides. For those who want to thoroughly think through for themselves what really goes into living well, what's just "icing," and what doesn't matter at all, a philosophical approach fits the bill.

The issues worth spending time on are the ones that actually come up in people's lives. To tackle a full range of issues, we'll need to acquaint ourselves with lots of different lives. We'll encounter Leo Tolstoy, Victor Frankl (a concentration camp survivor), the fourth-century desert saints, bereaved parents, mountain climbers, philanthropists, Wal-Mart employees, the cyclist Lance Armstrong, an escaped slave, and many more.

Looking at lives is also a way to test the plausibility of abstract theories. You can *say* that happiness is all that counts, or morality, or whatnot, but these claims become plausible (or implausible) only in light of the data of concrete lives. Sometimes the perfect test case is hard to find in the real world, so some of the people to be discussed live only in literature, movies, and the imagination. We'll talk about Neo from *The Matrix*, the butler in *The Remains of the Day*, and many other intriguing characters.

I began thinking about the main issues of this book during an unsettled period of my own life after my children were born. Having children brings about a change of focus. The sense of ultimate worth most people find in being parents calls into question previous assessments of value. You *did* want to leave your mark, or make a success of yourself, or make the most of a talent. Maybe these things are still important, and in your sleep-deprived, baby-besotted state, you're just losing your grip. Or maybe they aren't. Even as children grow older, life is never exactly the same, and you continue to think about what your priorities were, and are, and should be.

As a new parent, my focus shifted away from career and toward family, but also from the whole world to my own world. Before we became parents, my husband and I were active members of Amnesty International, the human rights organization. Our relationship got off the ground in a setting that directed our attention far beyond ourselves. At one memorable meeting, shortly after the 1994 Rwandan genocide, a Tutsi speaker talked about her memories of the massacre. At another meeting, we met a man who spent eight years on death row until he was vindicated and released. After our children were born, we continued to be card-carrying members, but it was just so hard to make it to the meetings. Had our priorities changed for better or for worse?

The shifts of attention from work to family, from the whole world to my world, trigger a new reflectiveness. So does the sense of vulnerability all parents experience. Before kids come along, it's not hard to muster the fatalism it takes to bicycle on busy roads, get wheeled into surgery, or consume raw oysters. But fatalism about your kids, or about your kids' Mom or Dad? It's out of the question. Are the things that matter most really frighteningly vulnerable to good and bad fortune – or is there some way around that conclusion? Being a parent makes you think about the matter, where before it might have seemed remote and abstract.

Whatever individual circumstances initially get us thinking, examining our own peculiar situation leads to thoughts about what is good and bad, possible and impossible, high priority and low priority, in a human life. This book will explore all those issues, considering what has been said, what could be said, and what stands up best in the face of evidence and argument.

I'll begin by talking about an especially vivid question – just what difference it makes that everything comes to an end. Just about everyone experiences a moment in life when transience seems connected to meaninglessness. My nine-year-old son occasionally likes to shock me with the utterance, "We're all going to die anyway, so what's the point?" I think he gets the question from the *Calvin and Hobbes* comics that he adores, but this is a thought that can be seriously troubling. Midway through his life, despite accomplishments anyone would envy, Leo Tolstoy began to have thoughts of transience that disrupted and transformed his life. He *had* to believe in an eternal God to restore his sense that his life was worth something. Is transience a genuine problem? Is religion the only solution? That's one of the basic questions this book tries to address. I broach it in Chapter 1 and come back to it toward the end of the book.

What must we aim for, to live good lives? The question is huge and it seems arrogant to even attempt an answer. To make any headway, you've got to ponder whether lives full of this or full of that always go well. Who am I to say? I discuss the whole business of being judgmental in Chapter 2, considering some very strange lives that will probably convince you that one life really isn't just as good as another. There are better and worse aims we can adopt. But what are they? I turn to the history of philosophy for possibilities, considering first the ancients and then the nineteenth-century Utilitarians in Chapters 3 and 4.

The building process starts in Chapter 5. What are we trying to build? When all is said and done, I don't think there is any such thing as "the good life," a single way of life that's better than any other. Whether it's a life of philosophical contemplation, or religious piety, or champagne and caviar, no specific way of life can claim to be uniquely good. Nevertheless, some lives do go better than others. Taken as a whole, a life sometimes has to be called good (or bad). What we want to build is an explanation: what makes some lives good and what makes others not so good? Without anointing any one specific lifestyle as "the good life", we can identify the features that good lives share. Conceivably, there could be just one such feature, but when we look at a rich variety of real lives, the conclusion we've got to reach is that there are many. In Chapter 5, I explore what these things might be. Is there one list of necessities that's relevant to every life? I come to that question in Chapter 6, placing it in the context of an emotional debate about the life prospects of people with severe disabilities.

Because I think there are many necessities, I think we inevitably have to cope with being pulled in many different directions. I explore what means we have for resolving conflicts in Chapter 7. It's tempting to think that morality has a pre-eminent place in life, that it's the sole important thing or the overriding thing. Is it? Examining the status of morality is the business of Chapter 8.

In Chapter 9, I come back to Tolstoy's crisis, and, more generally, the role of religion in living well. If you think of religion as a great divide, and you want to know which side I'm on, I'll let you know right now that my position is going to be (annoyingly?) diplomatic. There was something right and something wrong with Tolstoy's conviction that he could find no meaning in life without religion.

Chapter 10 wraps things up and ties a variety of loose ends. If there are necessary aims, are there also optional aims – things it's good to aim for but only if you want to? Where do the things we care about most fit in – taking care of our families, making art (if that's your passion), running marathons, cooking great food, making a positive difference in the world, expressing ourselves, learning about the universe we live in? Whether or not you're persuaded by my arguments, my hope is that you'll be drawn into the centuries-old debate about these ultimate questions.

Chapter 1

———— This Mortal World ————

Nothing lasts forever. The project you've worked on all year will be completed and forgotten in a flash. Some day you'll be gone, along with your children and your children's children. Even a book, a major artwork, or an important theory can make a splash and then fade into obscurity.

Thoughts like these can shape the way we live our lives. If you want to overcome transience, you might choose to focus your energy on whatever promises a longer-lasting result: home improvement, rather than a party; your marriage rather than temporary friendships; publishing a book instead of an article; getting to heaven rather than making the most of this mortal life.

But why make any of these choices? Is transience really any problem at all? Perhaps *you* react to the mortality of all things with complete indifference. Are you making a mistake?

LEO TOLSTOY FOUND IMPERMANENCE profoundly troubling. By the time he reached the age of 50, in 1878, he had earned fame and acclaim for *War and Peace* and *Anna Karenina*, he had amassed abundant wealth, and he had brought nine children into the world with his devoted wife. Nevertheless, as he lived and worked at his vast estate near Moscow, surrounded by his family, everything started to fall apart. The crisis was brought on by the thought that nothing lasts forever. People die, things decay, fame fades, great moments pass. "Sooner or later my deeds, whatever they may have been, will be forgotten and will no longer exist," he wrote in his autobiographical *Confession*. "What is the fuss about them?" These were no idle philosophical ruminations. "My life came to a standstill," Tolstoy wrote. He plunged into a depression, stopped writing, and withdrew from his family.

Why should life be worthless if nothing lasts forever? I can emotionally sympathize with Tolstoy's mood of despair. In a bad enough mood, I can find it pointless to put any energy into things that pass quickly – Thanksgiving dinner, a child's birthday party, even a vacation. But is there really no point to life if nothing we do has lasting significance? Intellectually, it's not so easy to understand Tolstoy's crisis.

There really seem to be loads of things with no lasting result, but undeniable value. A child spends an enjoyable hour building sandcastles at the beach. Nobody records the event and all memory of the event eventually disappears. How can it be denied that this small slice of the child's life is worth something? And come to think of it, why doubt that a quickly forgotten Thanksgiving dinner, or birthday party, or a great vacation, has some value?

Intimations of worthlessness seem to come from looking upon these events from a remote perspective. You imagine yourself a denizen of a future millennium. It's the year 10,000 and life as we know it has virtually disappeared. You look back at a special moment in the year 2000 and it's something of vanishing significance. What seemed vastly important at the moment now seems vastly unimportant.

But is hindsight, from such a distant point in time, really 20/20? Maybe from that far off, we actually can't see accurately. We are in the position of someone looking at an object from a great distance. What comes to mind is a scene from the movie *The Third Man*: looking down from the top of a Ferris wheel, a shadowy criminal, played by Orson Welles, remarks to a friend that the people below look like ants; they can't really be worth caring about. That's his excuse for selling watered-down vaccines on the post-war Viennese black market, and causing the suffering and death of innocent children. And it *seems* for a moment like he is right. But not for long. People aren't ants just because they look that way from afar. Likewise, an enjoyable hour at the beach isn't valueless just because it seems that way if it's imagined from the perspective of a time far, far in the future.

Was Tolstoy's crisis a result of adopting the year 10,000 perspective too often? Maybe – but there was more to it than that.

EACH OF US IS running out of time. The amount of future I'm going to get a chance to enjoy is getting smaller and smaller. And then, there's no way of making up for the diminishing future by revisiting the past. I can't take trips backwards and have a second helping of periods of time I particularly enjoyed. The human condition gives each of us the problem of our mortality, and doesn't mitigate the problem by providing any opportunities for time travel. If we dwell on it, we can be alarmed by the sense that the moments of our lives are a diminishing and non-recyclable resource.

We get used to the elementary facts about death and time. Once we lose our capacity to be shocked by them, it's interesting to think about how these facts are experienced for the first time. My own children were completely unaware of death until they were about three years old. An awful smell was permeating the house and the exterminator said it was coming from a dead squirrel trapped in a wall. I vividly remember my daughter saying, "People don't ever die, do they?" I thought honesty was the best policy and gently admitted that people do die some day ("when they're very, very old and they're ready" – no reason to cover all painful topics at the same time). Both my daughter and her twin brother found this fact devastating, much to my surprise.

Midway through his life, it's as if Tolstoy re-experienced a child's first awareness that someday she is going to be "discontinued." In his story "The Death of Ivan Ilyich," written soon after *A Confession*, he describes the terror of facing imminent death in gruesome detail. Ivan Ilyich becomes ill after a minor accident and soon realizes that he's sliding unstoppably toward the end. He simply can't come to terms with his predicament. "In the depths of his heart he knew he was dying but, so far from growing used to the idea, he simply did not and could not grasp it." Tolstoy agonized over his own mortality for many years, but could never take it in his stride.

Is it even possible to look at our mortality head on and accept it? An affirmative answer comes from a surprising place. Viktor Frankl was uprooted from his home in Vienna in 1942 and sent to a series of four concentration camps. A neurologist and psychiatrist, Frankl often found himself counseling prisoners at the brink of death. He encouraged them to find solace in the thought that the past is not nothing. Though his wife and parents were killed, he survived and wrote a detailed description of life in the camps, *Man's Search for Meaning*. In the book, he explains his conception of the past this way:

[I]n the past, nothing is irretrievably lost but everything irrevocably stored . . . Usually, to be sure, man considers only the stubble field of transitoriness and overlooks the full granaries of the past, wherein he had salvaged once and for all his deeds, his joys and also his sufferings. Nothing can be undone, and nothing can be done away with. I should say *having been* is the surest kind of being.

As long as I'm living I can take satisfaction in the events of my past, like the day I was married. Frankl's more radical suggestion is that when I'm gone, those events won't exactly disappear. Though now over, my wedding day is a frozen and unalterable part of the past. It will remain there, safe and secure, even after I'm gone.

But wouldn't it be better if the past were a permanent reality *and* we lived forever? No, Frankl says. Death is actually a blessing, because it gives us the urgency to get on with our plans and projects. Without the inevitability of dying some day, we would wile away our days in an eternity of procrastination. Why learn to play the guitar now if you can learn in a hundred years, or in a thousand . . .?

Frankl does not mean to deny that the Nazis committed terrible crimes by murdering millions of people. They forced upon their victims drawn-out deaths involving almost unimaginable suffering. They deprived them of years of their lives and inflicted devastating losses on their loved ones. Frankl's goal was to help people come to terms with just one critical element of their obviously terrible situation – the elementary fact of human mortality. By helping them accept *that*, he thought he could ease their pain.

I hope many prisoners were comforted, but fear some were not. These deaths were going to be terribly tragic, even if the elementary fact of death is not. When people die too young or with too much left undone, what has been stored in the "granaries" of the past is just not enough to constitute a complete human life. Ivan Ilyich could have found no comfort in Frankl's words. As he lies on his deathbed, ruminating about the way he's spent his life, he finds little to savor in his past. He has wasted his energies on maintaining appearances – indeed, he thinks he's dying because of a trivial accident that took place while he was hanging draperies (Tolstoy is ambiguous about the true diagnosis). His life was short and pointless and now the lights are about to go out. Having lived his life badly, nothing can help him but more time – which (to his horror) he doesn't have.

But what about Tolstoy? At the time of his crisis, he had already accomplished more than most people ever will. His own private granary was overflowing with golden grain. Tolstoy was a prime candidate to be comforted by Frankl's ideas. If we visualize the two of them in the same room, should we imagine Tolstoy the patient being comforted by Frankl the psychiatrist?

Tolstoy would have been a particularly challenging patient. Storing things in the granaries of the past may keep them alive – and keep us alive – in some nebulous sense, but can't possibly satisfy the strongest appetite for permanence; and Tolstoy had a very strong appetite. Besides, as hard as it is for us to grasp, Tolstoy had come to find little value in any aspect of his life; in his own mind, at least at times, he *was* Ivan Ilyich. Could he at least have appreciated death for the way it helps us get on with the things we want to do? Even that would have been a tough sell. Tolstoy didn't seem to need the deadline that death provides. He'd always worked and lived intensely, even when death was nowhere in his thoughts.

For most of us, the shock of confronting mortality gradually dissipates. An unforeseen death or a health crisis can briefly make us think about our mortality, but most of the time we're happy to allow a thick curtain to veil our inevitable end. Children learn to draw that curtain early on. It's now been six years since my children first learned about death. For many months they returned to the subject with an intensity that only grew. A particularly intense round of tears turned out to be the last of it. When the subject of death comes up these days, they don't dwell on it.

To fully understand why the fact of mortality had such a persistent grip on Tolstoy, we need to look at the matter from another angle.

THERE IS A LONG tradition in philosophy that sees transience as inherently negative and permanence as inherently positive. This view is expressed most fully and eloquently by Plato. Ten years before his crisis, Tolstoy learned Greek and read the classics, including Plato, untranslated. (He said the originals were "like spring-water that sets the teeth on edge, full of sunlight and impurities and dust-motes that make it seem even more pure and fresh," while translations were like "boiled, distilled water.")

Plato conceives the world around us as a pale imitation of a more glorious reality. We live in a world of ceaseless change, of becoming, that's accessible to our senses. But beyond the reach of our senses, there's an invisible world of being. The many beautiful things around us owe their beauty to the one imperceptible beautiful thing in that other world – what Plato calls beauty itself or the form of beauty. For each Many in the perceptible world of becoming (many tall things, many triangles, many chairs), there is a One in the other realm.

Change is an inherently negative trait of the world of becoming. The badness of change is a brute fact – there is no explaining it. It's not that Plato thinks transitory things and activities are devoid of all value. He doesn't adopt the Ferris wheel perspective from which everything seems worthless. There are good acts, good people, good books – all occupants of the world of becoming. Such things can even be imbued with a great deal of goodness. But they suffer from a fundamental metaphysical defect – as good as they may be, they are impermanent. One source of Tolstoy's crisis was an acute sensitivity to this "defect" (if it really is one). Since all his worldly accomplishments were transient, his life seemed hopelessly flawed.

Can we overcome transience? We're stuck "down" here in the realm of becoming; we can't live our lives in the superior realm of the unchanging. But Plato sees ways for us to reach in the direction of permanence. For one, you can do so intellectually. If you reflect on the nature of beauty itself (or goodness, or justice, or any other "One") and try to understand what it really is, then you are contemplating the permanent things in the realm of the forms. You don't actually become permanent yourself, but you get a kind of intellectual respite from ceaseless change. We can also try to conduct ourselves in a way that conforms to the form of justice, or create art that conforms to the form of beauty. We won't become permanent ourselves, but we can have the satisfaction of creating, so to speak, mirrors in which the permanent realm is reflected.

The hope of actually escaping death is expressed in one of Plato's greatest dialogues, *The Phaedo*. The setting of this dialogue is the prison cell where Socrates has been condemned to spend his final days; a jury has convicted him of blasphemy and corrupting the young. At the end of the dialogue Socrates drinks the hemlock, fulfilling the jury's sentence of death. Socrates, as Plato depicts him, soothes his grieving friends by explaining why death does not terrify him. Our souls, he says, have a chance of departing for the realm of the forms after death, depending on the life we have led. Devote yourself too much to bodily things while you live, and your soul will be too weighted down to escape your body and consort with the forms when you die; but live a philosophical life, contemplating the forms, and your soul will leave the world of becoming and dwell among permanent things forever. (Some commentators have questioned how serious Socrates – or Plato – is about this. Is he just comforting his distraught followers with a childish story? He does say, later in the dialogue, "No sensible man would insist that these things are as I have described them, but I think it is fitting for a man to risk the belief . . .")

We can only satisfy the craving for permanence if we live a life that's very different from the conventionally successful life. We must not be focused on the superficial glamour of good looks, money, and material possessions. We must not even be focused on our spouses and our children. Plato depicts Socrates as being exemplary in this regard, when he has him respond coolly to his wife and children when they come to the prison to see him just before his death.

If permanence must somehow be achieved in a life that's worth living, what recourse do we have if we can't quite bring ourselves to believe in Platonic forms? Many of the great world religions postulate permanent realities and ways of "connecting" to them. The earliest books of the Bible depict a covenant between the "chosen people" and an eternal God. By having a relationship to God and obeying his laws, there is the promise of a kind of escape from the flux of ordinary life, though not a way to survive death. The emphasis changes to overcoming death in the New Testament. Life everlasting is the "good news" and the promise of the Christian gospel. Buddhists seem to positively embrace impermanence, but even here, there's a Platonic element. The enlightened *arhat* is released from the cycle of rebirth but dissolved into the never-ending flux of being. Plato's path to permanence may seem obscure, but kindred routes are familiar to religious people everywhere.

TOLSTOY'S CRISIS WAS RESOLVED gradually. At first he turned to philosophy and science for a way out of his predicament, but he found no satisfying answers there. Then he turned his attention to the peasants on his estate. He wondered how they went on in spite of the realities of disease and death, and concluded that their religious faith was the key. As he worked in the fields by their sides, gradually, by a sort of osmosis, their faith was transmitted to him.

Tolstoy's original problem was a painful sense of transience, and the part of religion that interested him solved that problem. How did he get over the feeling that nothing matters? He writes:

Whichever way I put the question: how am I to live? the answer is always: according to God's law. Or the question: is there anything real that will come of my life? the answer is: eternal torment or eternal bliss. Or, to the question: what meaning is there that is not destroyed by death? the answer is: unity with the infinite, God, heaven.

Union with the infinite was the essence of faith, for Tolstoy, and he saw this element equally in every religious tradition. The rest of religious doctrine, for him, was just myth making, and he wrote about the stories of the Bible with undisguised contempt. ("[N]o other faith has ever preached things so incompatible with reason and contemporary knowledge, or ideas so immoral as those taught by Church Christianity. This is without mentioning all the nonsense in the Old Testament . . ."). A truculent critic of the Russian Orthodox Church, he was ultimately excommunicated.

Tolstoy's new-found faith changed his life. He became contemptuous of his famous novels and turned over their copyrights to his wife. Yes, great novels are relatively permanent, more permanent than dinner parties or Moscow balls; even more permanent than children. But they are not eternal. Returning to literature only sporadically, he began to devote himself to writing essays on religious themes. Now he despised the high society life the rest of the family enjoyed during sojourns to Moscow; he grew impatient with the clutter of children, teachers, servants, and visitors that surrounded him the rest of the year at the family's estate in the country. Intermittently, he gave up meat, alcohol, and sex. Later in life, Tolstoy would periodically abandon his family to help the poor during periods of famine or to briefly live in the austerity of a monastery.

To live "for permanence" means adopting a set of priorities and letting them guide life decisions. Depending on the sort of permanence we think possible, and the way we think it can be achieved, it might be to live as Socrates did, or as Tolstoy did after his conversion, but the craving for permanence can shape our lives even if we feel no hope of linking ourselves to other-worldly realities. The warriors of heroic sagas like the *Iliad* think it's worth it to die bravely on the battlefield, never to return to the warmth and security of family life, because fame will make them immortal. They take comfort in the belief that the memory of their great deeds will endure. In a more modern vein, we may be driven by the desire to leave behind books, artworks, musical masterpieces. Those with talent and initiative can make a lasting difference to the way a business is run, to the way a city is organized, to the prevalence of a disease, to the beauty of a park. Less ambitiously (but no less satisfyingly), we can leave behind children who go on living after we die, and (we hope) have their own children, and so on for many generations.

The craving for permanence can even drive us to focus on the past. By investigating your ancestry, you can feel like you're a part of a family that goes back hundreds of years. History, biography, and literature can also give us the sense of defying time. I recently spent a couple of weeks living in the ice age; later I traveled to nineteenth-century Russia, and then I stopped off in Rome during the first century. It was exhilarating getting out of the twenty-first century for a while and I am thankful to the novelist, the biographer, and the historian who gave me the opportunity.

For Tolstoy, the permanence of books and children and fame was really no permanence at all. He had these things in spades, and they gave him no relief from his sense of meaninglessness. Without transcendent realities – a supreme being, and an afterlife – there was no possibility of living a good and meaningful life.

In the United States today, where the vast majority of people give a central place to religion in their lives, there are plenty who agree with Tolstoy about the connection between God and life. Religion is the linchpin of a good life. If there is no God, we *ought* to be just as miserable as Tolstoy was during his crisis. This is the message of many popular Christian self-help authors – like Rick Warren, author of the mega-hit *The Purpose Driven Life*. Tolstoy's version of Christianity is worlds away, but he is the patron saint of the basic theme: if there is no God, our lives really are of no account.

It's harder to find overt signs of the non-religious focus on permanence. It sounds distinctly unmodern – pompous, even – to say you are motivated to write books by a desire to leave behind something permanent, or you want to have children so you can live on in your descendants. We don't often talk that way. But that doesn't mean we don't feel that way. I would like to think that when I am gone, my children and grandchildren will still be around. If I could take credit for a

War and Peace, I think I'd feel a lot better on my deathbed. But would it make sense to give feelings like these a big role, or even a small role, in charting my course?

Is it really vital to overcome transience, in some way, shape, or form? Later on we'll return to the topic of permanence and take a stab at some answers. We cannot begin to do so without first tackling more fundamental questions.

Chapter 2

Strange Lives

What makes a life good, and what are the non-critical bells and whistles? Is there just one necessary ingredient, or many, or perhaps even none? Is happiness all that counts, or are there other things with just as much value? Do all good lives have things in common, or are they as varied as can be? These are the kinds of questions this book tackles. To grapple with them means making judgments about lives. This one is flawed; what's it missing? That one is great; what makes it so impressive? But judging is fraught with peril. We're not supposed to judge.

Of course we do judge, all the time. If you've opted for teaching in public schools, after weighing high income against having a positive impact, you're not likely to be able to resist a moment's doubt about your sister, the investment banker. A working woman might have the occasional doubt about her stay-at-home neighbor, who has so much time for decorating. We judge all the time, but should we?

In some "enlightened" circles, it's assumed that human life takes myriad forms, none inherently better than the rest. The focus of a life can be God, family, work, war, art, athleticism, acquisition. There's no basis for judging some lives good and others bad. The argument for being non-judgmental could start in many places and proceed in many ways. The strand of it that seems most worth taking up stresses the sheer variety of ways of living, not only across different historical and cultural settings, but within one society. In the face of this striking diversity, you could give up altogether on the whole idea of right and wrong, good and bad. Or, instead of renouncing ethical truth, you could conclude that ethical truth is relative. There are truths for me and truths for you. Or perhaps: truths for us and truths for them. Each group with its own culture – the ancient Romans, the Mayans, today's Chinese – has its own set of truths. Wary of stumbling into racism and cultural imperialism, we especially want to avoid judging dramatically different people in far-away places.

The most prominent issues of ethics concern the way we treat others. Is killing always wrong? Is lying ever right? Another part of ethics concerns the way we live our own lives. Here there are questions of limited scope, like whether it's all right to take drugs or cover your body with tattoos. And then there are questions of wider scope, like how to live your life, what priorities make sense, what activities to fill your life with.

Relativism about the first type of question goes against the grain. Was it right for the Mayans to perform human sacrifices, just because their culture embraced this practice? Could a lie be all right just because the liar thinks so? It's when it comes to the broadest questions about the way we live our own lives that our inclination toward tolerance is strongest. It's tempting to think that the direction a person's life takes is not a moral or ethical matter at all, that we shouldn't even speak of "good" and "bad," "right" and "wrong," but of different tastes (to each his own!). At least we ought to give any ethical talk a relativistic twist. The career woman's life really is good – for *her* – and the stay-at-home mother's life is good too – for *her*.

All this is tempting, but we really can't reasonably cast the questions about the way we live out of ethics. It would be odd to attach ethical significance to the way we treat others, but none at all to the way we treat ourselves; we couldn't attach importance to the narrower questions about the way we treat ourselves and none to the broader questions about the way we run our lives. Ethical language – perhaps with a variety of nuances – is the right language for discussing all these issues.

Our reluctance to judge is well founded, but the fact is that relativism about ways of living would give cover to some awfully strange lives. After dwelling on that point for a while, we'll ask whether there's good reason to embrace either the cultural form of relativism or the extreme form that says each individual erects his own ethical truths. In fact, I think there's no good reason. But if we can resist the temptation of relativism, a daunting question has to be faced. How can you and I, without being priests, poets, or sages, make any headway on the character of a good life? To go forward without embarrassment, we'll need at least the outlines of an answer.

My favorite example of an alien way of living transports us far, far away, to the deserts of Egypt and Syria at the end of the fourth century. This is where Christian monasticism got its start. The first monks were hermits who chose creative ways to deny themselves the pleasures of the flesh. Tolstoy, as we saw, went in for a bit of asceticism, but he was a hedonist compared to these guys. You can't get any stranger than this account of the life of Simeon "Stylites" (his epithet is from the Greek for "pillar"), in W. E. H. Lecky's marvelous *History of European Morals*, written in 1869:

> He built successively three pillars, the last being sixty feet high and scarcely two cubits in circumference, and on this pillar, during 30 years, he remained exposed to every change of climate, ceaselessly and rapidly bending his body in prayer almost to the level of his feet. A spectator attempted to number these rapid motions, but desisted from weariness when he had counted 1,244.

Simeon aspired to greatness, and the society around him thought he had achieved it. Lecky writes:

> From every quarter pilgrims of every degree thronged to do him homage. A crowd of prelates followed him to the grave. A brilliant star is said to have shone miraculously over his pillar; the general voice of mankind pronounced him to be the highest model of a Christian saint; and several other anchorites imitated or emulated his penances.

Mark Twain incorporated Lecky's description of Simeon into his story *A Connecticut Yankee in King Arthur's Court*, but he figured the reader could only stand so many gory details. In a footnote he wrote, "This book not being a history but only a tale, the majority of the historian's frank details were too strong for reproduction." The details make it clear just how strange Simeon's life really was (if you had any doubt). I can't resist quoting further from Lecky:

> For a whole year, we are told, St Simeon stood upon one leg, the other being covered with hideous ulcers, while his biographer was commis-

sioned to stand by his side, to pick up the worms that fell from his body, and to replace them in the sores, the saint saying to the worm, "Eat what God has given you."

Simeon was one of many thousands of hermits living in the deserts, each with his (or her) particular personal style. One monk lived in a hole and made a point of eating just five figs a day. St Eusebius carried around a 150-pound iron weight, and then lived in a dried-up well for three years. And then there was a sect called the grazers, "who never lived under a roof, who ate neither flesh nor bread, but who spent their time forever on the mountain side, and ate grass like cattle."

The inspiration for the retreat into the desert seems to have been the time Jesus is said to have spent in the desert after his baptism. St Anthony, the first well-known hermit, is described by his biographer, Athanasius, as fending off demons in the manner of Jesus. The intense suffering that Simeon seemed to seek might have been meant to imitate the suffering of Jesus on the cross.

Some scholars say that it is no coincidence that extreme monasticism flourished in the years after the conversion of the Roman emperor Constantine in 313, when Christianity had become a mainstream religion. With opportunities for martyrdom disappearing, Christians looked for new ways of proving their devotion. If entry into heaven couldn't be secured by martyrdom anymore, the extreme sacrifices of asceticism were an alternative.

Scholars point out that the extreme lifestyle was not chosen only as a ticket to heaven or an act of imitation. The desert saints were actually aiming for earthly perfection. Their way of living sprang from ideas about what is required to live the very best life possible. The word "asceticism" comes from the Greek word *askēsis* – exercise or training. One sort of person the adjective *askētikos* applies to is an athlete. The ascetic and a marathon runner have in common discipline, and a particular kind of discipline as well – the discipline involved in ignoring physical desires. In the same way that a runner would like to stop, rest, and cool down, how intensely the ascetics must have wanted to get off the pillar, get out of the well, find shelter from the sun, eat something other than figs. Who knows – the ascetics could have felt a bit of competitiveness with each other and might have experienced something akin to a runner's high. It was all ultimately to a different end, of course, for these were athletes of a special kind – spiritual athletes.

For being hermits, the desert saints had a lot of visitors. Their desert dwellings were often just a few miles from cities and towns, so pilgrims didn't necessarily have far to go. A bas-relief dated to the year 500 shows Simeon atop his pillar with a pilgrim approaching him on a ladder. Because of their extreme discipline, the hermits were thought to have the power to perform miracles, and they were credited with healing the sick and saving lives. Publicized by travelogues written by several pilgrims, the hermits became an inspiration to Christians throughout the Roman Empire.

The desert saints lived up to their own conception of the best life, and also lived up to cultural standards. So no consistent relativist can admit to any doubts about this type of a life. But doubts are unavoidable. Sitting in wells, standing on pillars, grazing like a cow – these can't be good ways to live, can they?

STANDING ON A PILLAR for 30 years is not living well. That's our gut feeling. Are we wrong to feel that way? Overly judgmental? Intolerant? Narrow-minded?

Looking at things from a relativist perspective, the desert saints must be judged positively. The ethical norms they fulfilled might not be "true for" us, but they were "true for" them. So the relativist says. But the phrase "true for" is strange. We don't think claims about the color of the sky, or the geology of Mars, or even about evolution or the existence of God, can be true for one but not for all. So how could this even begin to make sense in the case of ethical norms?

A relativist might start to answer the question by drawing our attention to a puzzling aspect of ethical truth: the way it pushes and pulls us. Once we acknowledge that feeding hungry babies is right, if we hear the baby crying hungrily, we have to get up and feed the baby. One way to account for this pushing and pulling is by regarding ethics as a system of commands or rules. There are commands like "feed the baby" and "tell the truth." And then there are commands that deal very generally with the way we live our lives, commands like "resist physical impulses" or "develop your talents."

Commands are issued *by* someone and *to* someone. An individualistic type of relativism sees commands as being issued by me to myself. For cultural relativism, the commander is "the culture" vested in parents,

THE WEIGHT OF THINGS

teachers, courts, legislatures, etc. Commands are issued to everyone in a particular social group.

If living ethically is a matter of obeying commands, it's reasonable to ask why anyone is motivated to be obedient. What gives these commands any force? Well, if I don't follow my own rules, I will feel an uncomfortable sense of discordance – I will feel guilt. Or, if ethical rules are cultural, they are sanctioned by the approval and disapproval, or even the rewards and punishments, of those around us.

Since commands are directed to and binding upon specific people, the command conception gives some clear sense to the notion that certain ethical claims can be "true for" me, but not for you, or "true for" people in fourth-century Egypt, but not for people in twenty-first-century America. The desert saints were complying with the ethical claims that were "true for" them, i.e. the commands aimed at them. The relativist goes on to say that we mustn't be critical. The fact that those claims were "true for" them gives the claims, and the behavior, immunity from being challenged.

Is that the right way to look at ethical talk – is it all rooted in commands that apply variously to this population or that, or even to one individual at a time? This interpretation winds up taking the luster off of *all* ethical talk, including the sort of talk that says it's always wrong to perform human sacrifices. It forces us to approve of the Mayans, when we actually want to disapprove. But let's keep the focus on the talk that's central to this book. There's nothing we can say against the desert saints' model of the best life if we embrace relativism. That life was right for them – just not right for us. Are these relativist pronouncements plausible?

Not as the argument stands so far. When a claim is known to be *true*, there is no sense in challenging it. We don't waste our time challenging truths; they're true! But why grant the same immunity to moral ideas that are merely true for a person or a group? A moral principle that's "true for" a person is just one that is implicit in prevailing commands. It's the principle she's expected to follow. Why should any ideas – unless they're known in advance to be *true* – be immune from being examined, questioned, tested, and ultimately perhaps rejected? A relativist needs to give us some good reason for restraint.

A RELATIVIST MIGHT GET his restraint from a sense of unfairness. People can't transcend the standards that are "true for" them or their cultures, he might say. Simeon was rewarded both by the satisfaction of living up to his own ideals and by the esteem of the pilgrims. How can we judge Simeon's strange life when he had no reason to live any other life?

My reply would be that Simeon did actually have a reason to live differently. Ethical precepts rooted in Greek philosophy and still in the air in the fourth century would have told Simeon to satisfy bodily desires, but in moderation. Offered that advice, Simeon would have had plenty of reason to take heed. Imagine what a relief it would have been to come down off that pillar, to have a hot bath and sleep in a clean bed! Imagine how pleasant it would have been for the man on the fig diet to eat a piece of bread, and for the guy who lived in the well to satisfy his desire for light and fresh air.

It's hard to believe that the hermits never had a single doubt about their lives. The man sitting in the well for three years must have occasionally wondered whether this made sense. Simeon must have had an occasional doubt about the worth of standing on the pillar. Other ascetics living in the deserts at that time might have scratched their heads now and again, even if just because they envied Simeon's fame; they might easily have wondered whether showy feats of asceticism really had any worth.

Most people do struggle to figure out what they ought to regard as good and bad, right and wrong, true and false. There are few cultures that indoctrinate individuals so thoroughly with one way of thinking that there is no room at all for private reflection. There's clear proof of the possibility of intellectual change in the *Confessions* of St Augustine, the famous theologian who lived in North Africa and Rome from 354 to 430. As a youth and a young man St Augustine enjoyed a life of pleasure; his studies led him to accept a rival to fourth-century Christianity, Manichaeism; later he became a Platonist, but he changed his mind again and turned to Christianity; for a time he adopted the monk's way of living – but without the extreme seclusion or austerities of the desert saints. Throughout his life he moved from one understanding of Christian doctrine to another and yet another.

The story of the life of Siddhartha Gautama ("The Buddha") in the fifth century BC is another story of evolving notions about how to live, a story that involves first the embrace and then the rejection of asceticism. Siddhartha was born a prince in the foothills of the Himalayas and lived a life of luxury and pleasure, protected by his father from any awareness of suffering or struggle. On a rare excursion from the palace he caught a glimpse of real life and decided to renounce his life of privilege. He joined up with five ascetics and wandered about for six years, meditating, begging for the little food he allowed himself, and depriving himself in every way. He came to a point, at the age of 35, when he decided that asceticism was not the way to go and parted company with his five friends (to their annoyance). Legend has it that he sat all night under a tree and by morning experienced enlightenment. His awakening was then developed, over more time, into the teachings that are the foundations of Buddhism.

These were great thinkers, and perhaps great thinkers have a greater capacity for change than the rest of us. But ordinary people change their minds too. They *can* question their own way of living. When we have doubts about a way of living that's not our own, our doubts are not usually completely alien to the life we are judging.

The lifestyle of the desert saints wasn't popular for long. Extreme penances were soon replaced by more moderate ones. The solitary life of the monks gave way to communal monasticism. The focus on chastity and self-control gave way somewhat to other concerns, such as charity. Our doubts about standing on a pillar for 30 years could have been, at least to a degree, the doubts of the desert saints themselves.

SUPPOSE WE ALLOW OURSELVES our doubts about the lifestyle of the desert saints. How can we expect to discover anything that's true about the way a person should live, instead of just things that are true *for us?* How can we expect to discover any objective ethical truths?

That there *is* such a thing is the view of many of philosophy's best-known figures. Immanuel Kant, the German philosopher of the late eighteenth century, embraces the command conception of ethics, but he says there is one true ethical imperative. It binds all people equally, without regard to time or place. That imperative originates not from culture or local institutions, but from Reason itself. Kant's "Categorical Imperative" tells us each to act on general principles that we could wish everybody followed. On the other hand, the commands of God might be seen as the standard that must be consulted to make all ethical assessments. On the Kantian and the religious views, the command picture of ethics is on the right track, but cultural relativism is wrong. The same ethical commands apply to all.

A higher standard doesn't have to be thought of in command terms. Plato postulates a form of the Good in the separate and invisible realm of the forms (see Chapter 1). It's only by achieving knowledge of that separate reality that we can make objectively correct judgments about ethical matters. Aristotle sees human nature as a touchstone for determining what is ethical and what is not.

All of these philosophers recognize truths about how to treat others, but also about the way we live our own lives. Questions about how we should live don't reside outside of ethics proper, or even on the edge of town. They are pre-eminent for the Greeks, and certainly on any Bible-based version of the divine command theory, and still quite central for Kant.

All of these perspectives recognize a foundation for ethical truth, whether it's the dictates of reason, God's commands, the form of the Good, or human nature. On the other hand, it's not always true that philosophers *base* their insights on any foundation. The convincing and enduring ideas emerge by a process of sifting through ideas, following out their implications, testing them against examples and counterexamples. This is the process called "dialectic" that is so beautifully portrayed in Platonic dialogues.

Maybe one or other of the foundationalist views are correct, but this is as much as I will assume in this book: out of good reasoning or sometimes just sheer perceptiveness, moral truths emerge – ideas that are true not just for me or for you, for one culture or for another, but *true*. We know some things at this point: slavery is wrong; gratuitous cruelty is wrong; pleasure is better than pain; racial purity is a worthless ideal; money, fame, and power have no intrinsic value. Even some ideas that do not yet command universal agreement may be moral truths: animals deserve moral consideration, women should enjoy the same freedoms that men do, torture is always wrong.

To gain access to ethical truths, one must be prepared to think carefully, consider past ideas, listen to objections, ponder counterarguments, and take seriously the possibility that one is actually wrong, or will later be proven wrong. That brings us back to the preposterousness – alleged – of tackling such big questions as those of this book. In fact, we needn't be priests, poets, or sages to get started. We only need to be prepared to think.

THE WEIGHT OF THINGS

What is good thinking, what is bad thinking? What is the difference between ethical thinking and other kinds of thinking? What is ethical truth, and how is it different from other kinds of truth? All of these questions are buried under the suggestion that we need to think. And we'll let them remain so. The point is that it's OK to attack the question of how we should live; we need no credentials or superhuman powers to be in a position to begin.

Reasoning and reflecting about what it is to live a good life is a legitimate enterprise, but one that needs to be undertaken with humility. We are in a better position to make reasonable claims about what really has value the more we have open-mindedly acquainted ourselves with human lifestyles, past and present, and around the world. How would I do that? Perhaps by immersing myself in every way of life, living fully as a Tibetan monk for a couple of years, and then as a member of an Inupiat community, or maybe as the fourth wife of a Mormon patriarch; and on, and on, and on. The problem is that I'd never be finished, and all the discontinuity would leave me hopelessly confused. I can't really get myself into an ideal position from which to think about life. The best I can do is to admit that.

It's always possible that instead of attaining genuine insight, we're spinning out our personal and cultural biases. Philosophers who claim objective foundations for their moral positions, and those who reason and reflect ever so carefully, have sometimes been blinded by their times or their personal predilections. Plato says the ideal society is rigidly class structured and ruled by philosopher kings; Aristotle defends slavery; the Bible says nothing against slavery; Kant, in an obscure place, says that masturbation is an abomination worse than suicide. All we can do is think things through as best we can, in the hope that some of our conclusions will stand the test of further experience and reflection.

Understanding individual and cultural differences *is* important. For one thing, understanding makes us more astute judges. It's safe to say we are usually too quick to judge the neighbor with a different lifestyle or the sister who chooses a different career. The more we understand the desert saints, the more we can actually find some good in their lives. If discipline is good, they had it. If devotion is good, they had that too. If there really is a possibility of achieving eternal life after death, doing what it takes to achieve it makes sense.

Still, when all is said and done, there's something badly amiss with a life that's spent standing on a pillar or sitting in a well or grazing in a pasture (unless you're a cow). To say just why, we'll have to think through many questions about what makes a life go well.

Chapter 3

——— Reason and Luck ———

We want to know what makes a life good, what to aim for and what to make our first priority; what matters most and what doesn't matter at all. How can we begin to think about such big questions? A good warm-up before directly confronting them is a walk through history. We'll spend this chapter looking at ancient ideas, and the next on the leading modern views. I'm not going to agree with the ancient or modern views entirely, but I'm going to find in them a rich source of materials that I'll later put to use.

How to live was the paramount issue for philosophers in ancient Greece and Rome. As much as their world seems different from ours, their concerns were not so different. The ancients' ideas about the best life were always mingled with thoughts about who can have that life and who can't. Is a good life just for the lucky and privileged? How much do I control my well-being?

The theme of personal control is explored in Greek tragic poetry. All is well in the life of Oedipus, until he just happens to quarrel with a man at a crossroads and the man winds up dead. That would have been water under the bridge, except that the man happened to be his biological father. Oedipus continues to Thebes, where he meets and marries the queen. Not a problem at all – until it turns out that the queen is his biological mother. A small turn of events, a coincidence, an accident of timing, a chance encounter, can all change the course of a life. Sophocles hardly gives the story a happy ending.

The poets agreed that happenstance can ruin our lives. The problems that beset the heroes of the *Iliad* can't be turned around. When Agamemnon leads a thousand ships against Troy, there's no wind to help them set sail across the Aegean. The gods offer their help, on one condition: Agamemnon has to offer up the life of his daughter; the usual animal sacrifice is not sacrifice enough. Either he's going to let down the whole Greek battalion or he's got to fetch the girl from home, with a false story that she's going to marry Achilles. The terrible story is told in not one but many plays by Euripides and Aeschylus. Suffice it to say that the tragedians don't throw Agamemnon a rope.

If the issue of happenstance were raised only by such exotic circumstances, we'd have no need to worry about it. We're not likely to wind up accidentally killing Dad and marrying Mom; or to be forced to choose between a child and a good breeze. But the threat of misfortune hovers over us every day. Six months ago, on the way home from teaching a class, I noticed a group of people standing by a tree that was surrounded by heaps of flowers. The scene was immediately recognizable as the aftermath of a fatal accident. The next day, I learned that a six-year-old girl had been killed by a high school senior driving to school on the day of his eighteenth birthday. She had been walking to school with her mother and a younger sibling. The driver had stopped at the stop sign, but had turned left and hit the girl. There are still ornaments on the tree – recently there were balloons (for her birthday?) – reminding me regularly to wonder what life must be like for the parents of that girl. I wonder also about the driver (he was indicted recently for vehicular manslaughter).

The ancient poets thought that our well-being was tenuous and vulnerable, but we might expect something different from the ancient philosophers. We'll see if they deliver.

THE MOST COMPREHENSIVE AND systematic work of ancient ethics is Aristotle's *Nicomachean Ethics*, generally taken to be a set of lecture notes. Aristotle gave his lectures on ethics to an audience of wealthy young men at the Lyceum, a gymnasium just outside the walls of Athens. This was the place where democracy first flourished and philosophy was practically born. A city of perhaps half a million people, it shouldn't be imagined as primitive just because it reached its high point in the fifth century BC. Of course, great art and architecture were displayed in public buildings like the Parthenon. But everyday living was also quite civilized. People lived in attractive, attached two-story buildings with wood floors, shuttered windows, and painted plaster walls. Possibly a third of the population was made up of slaves, who assisted free Athenians in all of their endeavors. Slave labor created leisure and was no doubt one factor that made it possible for the Athenians to devote so much time to philosophy, poetry, and their democracy.

Aristotle was deeply at home in Athenian culture, but was never a citizen. He hailed from Macedon, where his father was a physician. During his first 20 years in Athens, he was the most famous student of Plato. After leaving and spending some time back in Macedon as tutor to Alexander the Great, he returned to Athens and headed his own philosophical school for 10 years; this school spawned yet others, which continued through the Hellenistic period and into the second century AD. One of those successor schools started off, soon after Aristotle's death, in the Stoa – an Athenian building named for its painted porch; much later, Stoicism came to be the predominant philosophy of both emperors and slaves in Rome.

Based on his lecture notes, we can see that Aristotle would have started off his lectures on ethics by claiming that all people aim at one "final end" (*telos*) – the good. The point of understanding the nature of the good is both personal and political. He expects the study of the good to help his students achieve the good in their own lives. But the point of the state is to produce good lives for all, so better knowledge of the good will be useful to them as they get involved in politics (and most of them will).

Aristotle also expects quick agreement on what the good *basically* amounts to. He says it is *"eudaimonia."* "Having it all," "doing well," and "flourishing" have all been suggested, though "happiness" remains the most widely accepted translation. As Aristotle's account of *eudaimonia* unfolds, it becomes clear that "happiness," taken as a mere feeling, would be a misleading translation.

What exactly is *eudaimonia*? A clue, Aristotle says, is that our final end must lie in doing what is most characteristic of a human being. Surely there is something a human being does, just because he is a human being. He points out that humans share sheer life with plants and we share our senses with animals, so our function can't be living or perceiving. Aristotle says we are doing our characteristic work, as human beings, when we are actively reasoning.

Later on in the *Ethics*, the notion that our good must consist of doing what we *uniquely* do is dropped, so let's not make too much of it (he later says actively reasoning is something the gods do too). The underlying idea is not so much about exploiting our unique traits but about heading in the direction we naturally tend to go. To live as well as we can, we don't have to mold ourselves in some way that goes against the grain. The good life is an unforced life. This aspect of Aristotle's thought is nicely captured in the translation of *"eudaimonia"* as "flourishing," a word that suggests a similarity between a person living well and a thriving plant.

We can readily see what Aristotle would find glaringly flawed about a man living on a pedestal for 30 years. Simeon Stylites' life was like the most tortured topiary in a formal garden; he lived a life that was in all respects forced and distorted. The grazers, the sect that adopted the practice of living like grazing animals, chose a topiary-like life as well. What would have been unforced for a herd of cattle must have been entirely forced for those tireless hermits.

It's clear that Aristotle would be appalled by the desert saints' unnaturalness, but let's not get the wrong impression of what it would mean to live naturally. Aristotle's view calls to mind a variety of pearls of contemporary wisdom, but what is he really saying? Is it "Back to nature"? No, our home is in the civilized places where reason can develop. Is it "Be yourself"? Well, yes, but with the proviso that it takes effort and practice to fulfill our nature as rational beings. Furthermore, being me and being you are much alike; we share the same tendency toward reason. Is it "Be all that you can be"? That's better than "Be yourself," because there are other things that come naturally to us, such as eating, sex, sleeping, but we must develop the best part of our nature.

Where will we wind up if we cultivate the full flowering of our natural capacities? If the perfect rose is like this or that, what does the perfect human life look like? Aristotle argues that a human being who fulfills his nature will have *aretē* – excellence, or virtue – when it comes to the rational activity of his soul. He will use reason well both in the practical sphere and in the intellectual sphere.

Does Aristotle picture all humans who fulfill their nature well as simply doing *whatever* they do in life *with* ethical and intellectual virtue? Or does he picture such people as being engaged in similar activities? The phrase "the good life" suggests a quite specific way of living, not just some basic elements that can be present in diverse lives. The phrase comes from Aristotle and so it's not surprising that he *is* recommending a specific way of living (actually, two). The very best lives belong to the philosophers, and though in some minimal sense we can all be philosophers, in Aristotle's sense, we are not. The philosophers are those highly educated theoreticians of timeless truth who study the necessities of logic, science, and metaphysics. They certainly will have the moral virtues, but with all the time they devote to contemplation, they don't make the fullest possible use of them. The second-best lives belong to those who make the most of the practical virtues, and that's only possible "in politics or war"; though, again, in some weak sense we all can live a bit of that life by conducting our affairs with virtue, Aristotle has in mind participation in affairs of state, with a period of military service.

If you want to dilute Aristotle's view and make it a theory not so much of "the good life," with all the overtones of specificity, but of "a good life," you wind up with the claim that a good life for human beings, whatever the day-to-day content, makes excellent use of reason, both when it comes to learning and understanding and when it comes to practical affairs. "The good life" that Aristotle really has in mind is accessible to very, very few people; in some cultures, that life is not even conceivable. "A good life," on the diluted "neo-Aristotelian" conception, is far more attainable. Still, both conceptions put enormous emphasis on reason. Does Aristotle emphasize reason too much?

EVEN WITHIN ARISTOTLE'S REFINED audience, steeped in a 100-year-old philosophical tradition that venerated reason, there must have been a few students who wondered why reason should be so central to living a good life. How could ethical virtue or intellectual virtue be *that* important? Without sticking around for Aristotle's lectures on the virtues (they fill most of the *Nicomachean Ethics*), the audience would have been baffled. Once we see what Aristotle thinks the virtues are, we can see how having them might promote the kind of life we want to live.

What, then, are the virtuous ways of feeling and acting? In Book II of the *Ethics* Aristotle presents his famous doctrine of the mean. Ethical virtue is always a mean between two extremes. The person who is brave governs fear and confidence so that he feels them to an intermediate degree. Having too much fear is a vice (cowardliness), and having too little fear is a vice as well (rashness). Moderation is another mean between extremes. Bodily pleasures are to be sought and enjoyed not too much and not too little, but moderately. We don't want to be gluttons, but we don't want to be anesthetized either. Another familiar-sounding virtue is generosity; the mean lies between spending too much and spending too little. But the spending needn't be on others. Spending too much or too little on yourself is just as bad. Truthfulness is a surprise. It's not a virtue exactly concerned with lying or keeping secrets. Truthfulness is the virtue of being honest about oneself; the corresponding vices are being boastful and being self-deprecating. Justice is the virtue concerned with fair distributions.

Virtue has much to do with the modulation of feelings. But it's not a simple matter of keeping our emotional dial set within a middle range, something that would hardly be an achievement of reason. This passage conveys the complexity of what it is to choose the mean:

> We can be afraid, for instance, or be confident, or have appetites, or get angry, or feel pity, and in general have pleasure or pain, both too much and too little, and in both ways not well. But having these feelings at the right times, about the right things, toward the right people, for the right end, and in the right way, is the intermediate and best condition, and this is proper to virtue.

Once a person has attained the ethical virtues, unruly appetites no longer trouble him. This makes him the master of his affairs. When he's dealing with his wife or his children or his slaves, he can't be pushed to excessive anger. If he's on the battlefield he's not overcome by fear, but neither does he rashly throw himself into the wrong situations. He's not losing control over himself at the drinking parties the Athenians enjoyed, nor cowering at home in fear of participating in them. He's a person who shares his path in life with friends who are heading in the same direction. He acts moderately but appropriately in all the circumstances of his everyday life.

A virtuous life will normally be enjoyable. Virtue is its own reward – it gives us stability and enjoyment.

> Actions in accord with virtue are pleasant by nature, so that they both please lovers of the fine and are pleasant in their own right. Hence these people's life does not need pleasure to be added as some sort of extra decoration; rather, it has its pleasure within itself.

Aristotle is careful to be clear that pleasure is not an extra requirement, separate from virtue, but it is alien to him to contemplate a person having a great life but not a pleasant life. Happiness in the sense of sheer pleasure is important, but it's not our end in its own right. It comes along with virtue "for free."

With all of that as an explanation of what it is to possess ethical virtue, it's not as surprising that Aristotle gives such a key role to virtue in his account of the good life. But does he really mean to say virtue is *all* we need to live well? When Aristotle sets out his account of the good life, at first all focus is on virtue. He writes: "And so the human good proves to be activity of the soul in accord with virtue, and indeed with the best and most complete virtue, if there are more virtues than one." But then the plot quickly thickens. Aristotle writes:

> Nonetheless, happiness [*eudaimonia*] evidently also needs external goods to be added, as we said, since we cannot, or cannot easily, do fine actions if we lack the resources. For, first of all, in many actions we use friends, wealth, and political power just as we use instruments.

This may seem innocuous. If we think of virtue as a condition of the soul, then we will read Aristotle as saying that good people without resources simply don't get as many chances to exercise virtue. They're still good, and their goodness can still make their lives good. However, when we consider another aspect of the way that Aristotle conceives of virtue, the idea that we need external goods to do fine things takes on a new cast. Aristotle says that brave people do brave things and generous people do generous things. Bravery is not just a disposition to do and feel things should the opportunity ever arise. If that's so, when circumstances prevent a person from acting virtuously, she can't necessarily still be credited with virtue. If we need external goods to do fine things, that means we need them in order to *be virtuous*.

Aristotle goes on to make even more of a departure from his first characterization of *eudaimonia*:

> Further, deprivation of certain [externals] – for instance, good birth, good children, beauty – mars our blessedness. For we do not altogether have the character of happiness [*eudaimonia*] if we look utterly repulsive or are ill-born, solitary or childless; and we have it even less, presumably, if our children or friends are totally bad, or were good but have died.

It turns out that many of the things most people want (today and in Aristotle's time) – wealth, beauty, friends, children – actually *are* inherently important! He *does* only say that the lack of these things "mars our blessedness." "Marring" is not the same as destroying. However, the admission is significant.

This layer of Aristotle's thinking may strike you as being common-sensical, or you may find it disappointing. It would be uplifting to think that however poor you are, however ugly, however friendless, however childless, you still have a chance to have all that truly matters. Aristotle doesn't say that.

There were ancient philosophers who defended the uplifting view, just not Aristotle. In his greatest dialogue, *The Republic*, Plato depicts a very long conversation between Socrates and Plato's own brothers, Glaucon and Adeimantus. Glaucon draws a vivid picture of two dia-metrically opposed lives. One person is perfectly good, but lives in per-fectly awful circumstances. His situation is so awful that he even has a false reputation for being evil. Nothing is going right for him except his inner goodness. The other person is perfectly evil, but his circumstances are just perfect. He has everything he wants and he even has an unde-served reputation for goodness. Glaucon challenges Socrates to prove that the good man is better off, despite appearances. Yes, he *is* better off, argues Socrates (probably here voicing Plato's own position). Virtue is not only its own reward, but it is so rewarding that it makes all else unnecessary. How can this be? The very long discussion of justice "writ large" in the ideal city is an argument by analogy that Plato uses to show that a person with a just (good, virtuous) soul is supremely happy. Would the just person be any better off if his external circumstances were improved? Plato seems to think not – he is already supremely happy, thus there is no room for improvement.

Plato's view is beautiful, high-minded, and surely an inspiration to anyone stuck in a bad situation. But to Aristotle, it's just plain silly. He makes that clear in Book VII of the *Nicomachean Ethics*:

> [A]ll think the happy life is pleasant and weave pleasure into happiness, quite reasonably. For no activity is complete if it is impeded, and happi-ness is something complete. That is why the happy person needs to have goods of the body and external goods added [to good activities], and needs fortune also, so that he will not be impeded in these ways. Some maintain, on the contrary, that we are happy when we are broken on the wheel, or fall into terrible misfortunes, provided that we are good. Whether they mean to or not, these people are talking nonsense.

It takes some work to reconcile this passage with the one quoted earlier, in which Aristotle says we don't need pleasure as an extra decoration, but derive it from virtue. But the idea is reasonably clear. The key idea is that happiness is complete. When we have it, we're not impeded. And we don't have unconstricted, unforced, well-rounded, total happiness just by being internally virtuous. Things in the world outside of our souls must cooperate. Yes, virtue is its own reward. But (perhaps Aristotle is thinking) we don't fully experience that reward when we are beaten down by poverty, disfigurement, or a tragic loss. And besides, many things other than virtue can provide us with pleasure. To "have it all" – to have complete happiness – we can't be deprived of the pleasure of watching our children grow up, enjoying the material comforts that money can buy, and so on.

Where does the truth lie – with Aristotelian common sense or Plato's more uplifting position? Let's bring the two views to bear on the real-world tragedy at the beginning of this chapter.

WHAT WOULD ARISTOTLE, TURNED grief counselor, say to the unlucky parents who lost their six-year-old daughter, and to the young man who accidentally killed her? If external goods are ingredients of *eudaimonia*, the parents could be debarred from *eudaimonia* in a direct way. Must this be the decisive loss that costs them all chances of living a good life? Aristotle certainly doesn't think there's any guarantee that they can recover. If these people were to say, "Our lives will never be the same," he might nod his head in agreement. Aristotle will be no more optimistic if he counsels the driver, who might be hoping to hear him say, "I know that you are a good person, I know that you value life and never wanted to hurt that child. Really, you are no different from any other driver who is momentarily inattentive." Aristotle can't quite say that. It's true that virtuous people sometimes find themselves in situations that stop them from behaving virtuously. We wouldn't want to judge a person's character entirely based on one episode. But since being virtuous is a tendency to act in certain ways, actions are significant. If the driver feels some doubt about whether he is quite the good person he thought he was, I don't think Aristotle will try to rescue him from that doubt.

Plato, on the other hand, would encourage these parents to see that they have the power to remain happy and live good lives, so long as they preserve the virtuous state of their own souls. Leaving it at that, Plato's position is too abstract to be convincing. He would make a lousy grief counselor if he couldn't explain just what virtue has to do with overcoming grief. Instead of trying to extract the pieces of that explanation from *The Republic*, we'll turn to a later school of thought that took much the same position as Plato on virtue and happiness – Stoicism. The Stoics were far more concerned than Plato was with translating abstract philosophical ideas into useful advice for people dealing with the problems of everyday life.

Stoic ideas come down to us in fragments collected by later philosophers. The most sustained Stoic philosophizing appears in the later, less original writings of Cicero (first century BC), Epictetus (first century AD), and Marcus Aurelius (second century AD). The Stoic philosophy became, through the ages and even today, the helpmate of all, from overstressed leaders to people of limited means, the disabled or unattractive, people stuck in low-wage jobs, inmates and prisoners of war, and grieving parents.

The starting point for Stoicism, as for Aristotle, is the notion that we all aim at some good, and the Stoics agree with Aristotle that it is *eudaimonia*. Like Aristotle, the Stoics believe the virtues are central, and they recognize both moral and intellectual virtues. But for them, nothing else has intrinsic value; nothing else really matters.

What if you are wholly virtuous but you're stuck in a terrible situation? Despite the fact that the Stoics don't officially count feelings of happiness as good or feelings of misery as bad, it is important to them to show that the person who fully has the virtues will not in fact be miserable. She will achieve a tranquil state of mind, though we shouldn't expect her to bubble over with mirth. How will she achieve it? Well, one of the virtues she has will be wisdom, and her wisdom will enable her to look at ordinary situations in a different way than the average person does.

How will she look at things? Detailed practical advice is offered in the *Handbook* of Epictetus, essentially a first-century self-help book. Of the 53 short sections of the book, a number advise us to adopt certain general attitudes. We are to recognize that it's not the world as it actually is that affects us, but the way we think about it. We are to realize that we have the power to think about situations as we choose to. We are to focus our energies on what we can control (often, just the way we think about things) and ignore what is beyond our control (often, things "out there"). If we adopt all of these attitudes, we are supposed to be able to maintain tranquility come what may, even in the face of the loss of our own child. In that tranquil state, there's nothing that can overwhelm us and subvert our attention from living a virtuous life, which is all that ultimately counts.

Epictetus offers lots of advice for dealing with specific situations. Are you working toward some ambitious goal? Then figure out what you need to do to succeed, and do it, without complaining! Do you get immensely irritated by other drivers (in his example, it's people at the public bath)? Then before you get on the road, remind yourself that you don't just want to drive somewhere, but you want to maintain your equanimity. Do your children irritate you when they leave toys all over the house (in his example, it's your slave spilling the oil or stealing the wine)? What's it worth to try to stop this? Is it worth giving up your tranquility?

There is ample advice in the *Handbook* for dealing with the death of a child – an experience that was obviously as painful in the first century as it is today:

> What upsets people is not things themselves but their judgments about the things. For example, death is nothing dreadful (or else it would have appeared dreadful to Socrates), but instead the judgment about death that it is dreadful – that is what is dreadful.

But when your own child dies, how do you make yourself *feel* that it is not dreadful?

> If you are fond of a jug, say "I am fond of a jug!" For then when it is broken you will not be upset. If you kiss your child or your wife, say that you are kissing a human being; for when it dies you will not be upset.

Getting rid of the sense that a child is *my* child, and bringing myself to think of him as just *a child* is supposed to take me a long way toward being able to cope with loss. A similar idea appears in this passage:

> Someone else's child is dead, or his wife. There is no one would not say, "It's the lot of a human being." But when one's own dies, it is, "Alas! Poor me!" But we should have remembered how we feel when we hear of the same thing about others.

The point is that there really is no difference between my child dying and a neighbor's child dying, so a wise person will respond to the two in the same way. There is still more advice for how to maintain equilibrium in the face of death:

> Never say about anything, "I have lost it," but instead, "I have given it back." Did your child die? It was given back. Did your wife die? She was given back. "My land was taken." So this too was given back. "But the person who took it was bad!" How does the way the giver asked for it back concern you? As long as he gives it, take care of it as something that is not your own, just as travelers treat an inn.

Plato and the Stoics make good living a thing of adamantine strength. The most awful things that are thrown at the good person can't damage his life. Martha Nussbaum, the prolific philosopher and classicist, draws the contrast between Platonic and Stoic ideas about the good life, and Aristotelian ideas, with characteristic expressiveness. For Aristotle, a good life is more plant-like than rock-like. A life replete with virtue is not "something hard and invulnerable," Nussbaum writes, but has "the fragility, as well as the beauty, of a plant." You need water, soil, sun, and yes, you can be crushed. Aristotle accepts the reality of human need, vulnerability, and limited control. Plato and the Stoics don't.

OVER THE CENTURIES, MANY people have been helped through troubles large and small by reading Epictetus' *Handbook*. Admiral Jim Stockdale studied Epictetus in graduate school before becoming a fighter pilot in Vietnam. He was shot down in 1965 and spent the next five years as a prisoner of war in Hanoi. He gives much credit to Epictetus for his ability to endure relentless torture and years in solitary confinement. During his imprisonment he took to heart the pithy advice of the manual – nothing is valuable but virtue; nothing controls how you feel but your own state of mind; nothing has power over you but the way you look at the world.

If all this is really true, it would help us in the midst of our troubles, and also help us go through life with a sense that our well-being is within our control. Epictetus must have an initial appeal to any new parent first encountering that sense of vulnerability I described in the introduction. A baby is born, and everywhere we look there are small forces that could totally undermine us: an unlocked cabinet, or a piece of candy that could go down the wrong way, or an unwashed piece of lettuce. If Epictetus is to be believed, none of these things can harm us. They can't even *really* harm the baby. (Yes, they can kill him, but death does no real harm, according to Stoicism; the only thing that's genuinely bad is being a bad person.)

Epictetus is the forerunner of today's cognitive therapists, who emphasize the impact of our thinking on our emotional lives. There's also an intriguing connection between Stoicism and Buddhist counsel on avoiding suffering by changing our psychological orientation. The origin of suffering, according to the second of the Four Noble Truths, is thirst or craving. If we can still our strivings, we can find contentment in our situation as it is. Thinking differently is the key to desiring differently. A rather ghoulish example is this cure for physical attraction:

> We develop attachment to things because we see them as attractive. Trying to view them as unattractive or ugly counteracts that . . . When you start to analyze this attachment, you find that it is based on viewing merely the skin . . . Now let's analyze human skin: take your own, for example. If a piece of it comes off and you put it on your shelf for a few days, it becomes really ugly. This is the nature of skin.

Would you really want to cure yourself of an excessive attraction at the cost of finding skin (everyone's) disgusting? Maybe not. But it's true that cognitive cures for everyday problems are frequently useful. Epictetus really does offer lots of good advice. Each time I read him, I find myself better able to face annoyances with equanimity (for as long as I keep his advice in mind). There's plenty of calming wisdom in the popular works of the Dalai Lama and other Buddhist sages, like the very articulate and readable Vietnamese teacher, Thich Nhat Hanh.

But I agree with Aristotle when he says we cannot live an entirely good life "on the wheel." The misfortune of losing a child cannot be overcome by seeing the child as "a child" rather than "my child"; the cruelties of a prisoner-of-war camp cannot be undone by looking at them in the right way. We may be able to lessen the damage the world does to us by controlling our response to it, but we can't avoid that damage altogether. We can value Stoic wisdom while also saying what is obvious: driving carelessly and killing a child is a disaster; torture is a bad thing, no matter how much control over the pain a victim can muster. If these things weren't so, it wouldn't be so important for the driver to become virtuous and slow down; for the torturer to become virtuous and stop. I think we all know, deep down, that what happens in the world matters even if we are disciplined about what happens in our minds.

If Aristotle is correct about our vulnerability, that's not to say he's *all* right. He is also perhaps too pessimistic. As we read Aristotle, we get the impression that he has some tendency to think of external goods as being less within our control than they are. We are dealt our hand, and for some it precludes access to the best life. We certainly can't escape being born slave or non-slave, Athenian or non-Athenian, male or female. If we don't have wealth, we might not be able to acquire it. If we're "utterly repulsive" there's not a lot we can do about it. What happens to our children is pretty unpredictable.

The Stoics actually display a similar strain of resignation about external events. And that may be why they wish to discount them. They think we have to twist and turn to form the right state of mind because we can't (or often can't) change the way things are. The solution is always to fix myself, not to fix the situation that (at least on the surface) is responsible for my problem.

A sense of inevitability about the events of the world is possibly an effect of living in a world with a rigid social structure, a world without advanced medicine and technology. And maybe it's also a product of the idea, so prevalent in Greek drama and poetry, though not officially in philosophy, that the impersonal forces of Necessity, Luck, and Fate are not to be resisted.

Aristotle and the Stoics have the philosophical tools to see things in another way. The moral and intellectual virtues that they stress so much can be enlisted to help us acquire and safeguard external goods. A prudent mother crosses the street with great caution. A prudent driver doesn't rush to school in the morning, placing the lives of pedestrians at risk.

Still, as hard as it is to admit, we cannot exercise perfect control. "Shit happens," as the bumper sticker says. Even the most prudent people do lose children to accidents. People who plan carefully and work hard lose jobs or never get good jobs to begin with. There is another layer of pessimism in Aristotle concerning the aftermath of external misfortune. In Aristotle's vision of things, when bad things happen to a person, they may never be the same; their "blessedness is marred" for good. This meshes with the story lines of Greek tragedy. After Oedipus inadvertently kills his father and marries his mother, he doesn't find a twelve-step program, or meet up with a counselor who reassures him it was all a big mistake. He doesn't transcend the experience and become wiser for it. No, he dashes out his eyes. Agamemnon, forced to choose between the good of his own child and the good of all the Greeks, offers up the child as a human sacrifice. After 10 years of fighting against Troy, he returns home victorious. And what awaits him? A wife who is not especially understanding about the way her husband resolved his dilemma; in a word, a bloodbath. There is no happy ending, for anyone.

There is another way that things can go, a story line that we don't see in Greek literature and that Aristotle doesn't recognize as a possibility. A terrible thing occurs, and it transforms a person so that he or she goes on living in better, more meaningful ways. The biographies we love to read often tell this kind of story. In his autobiography *Every Second Counts*, Lance Armstrong, the seven-time Tour de France winner, says that having testicular cancer wound up being a better thing for him than all of his bicycling successes. After the illness, he went on to create a foundation that helps people cope with life after cancer and he found a real sense of purpose in his life.

The possibility of transformation does not mean that death and disease aren't bad things after all. We really do want to cure cancer, even at the cost of the personal transformations that can result from it. We want to prevent another September 11, even if it means no more survivors whose lives are given meaning by their losses. The point is that a person who suffers a serious and clearly undesirable loss needn't find the rest of his life moving downhill. Not everyone who suffers a devastating misfortune becomes an Oedipus or an Agamemnon.

COULD WE, WITH ANY plausibility, say that transformation is *always* possible? The ornaments hanging from that tree, commemorating the young girl's death, are not just any ornaments. They are crosses. I don't know the parents, but that gives me some small clue to their state of mind. The narrative of transformation is especially at home in Christianity. The ultimate transformation story depicts Jesus suffering and dying on the cross, and then being resurrected, giving believers the possibility of eternal life. The New Testament message is that death can transform the earthly human being into an eternal incorporeal being. From that perspective, the girl is now in a better place. The parents have not suffered the tragedy of seeing their daughter's life end completely. Their grief must be, from this perspective, about missing her, not about her life being over.

Does Christianity offer a hopeful narrative of transformation not only about the girl's death, but about the survivors' grief as well? That's less clear. Jesus heals the sick and raises the dead; he does not counsel sick people and grieving relatives to find meaning and purpose in misfortune. We would have to look at multiple sources, some outside of Christianity, to explain today's common conviction that "everything happens for a reason," that every terrible experience can lead to a greater good.

We want to believe that recovery and transformation are *always* possible, but surely that is too simple to be the honest truth in every case. The tragic picture is *sometimes* the right picture. In the first place, not every trouble with externals is a disaster that hits all at once, devastates and disrupts. External trouble can mean chronic poverty, or powerlessness, or ill health. Yes, there is transformative potential even there. But for each person transformed in some way by chronic problems, there are many who simply live with them, and others who slowly come undone.

And then, when disaster does strike suddenly, there isn't always a chance for renewal. Being a parent of a child who "goes bad" (as Aristotle puts it) creates less potential to be transformed positively than having a child who tragically dies. If you are the parent of the Columbine killers, or the September 11 hijackers, or Timothy McVeigh, shame will drive you to seclusion, while the parents of victims meet with commissions, plan memorials, and share their sorrow with other survivors.

To expect transformation out of every disaster is naïve. But to assume that every disaster puts a person's life on a downward trajectory is too pessimistic. A complete picture recognizes that different lives tell very different stories.

It's easier to swallow Aristotle's view that externals do matter when we embrace the non-Aristotelian (and generally non-ancient) view that we can work to promote and preserve external good fortune; and that when bad things happen anyway, we can use those experiences in ways that take us in positive new directions. But let's avoid being Pollyannas. Some people – really, many people – are unlucky in externals, and through no fault of their own wind up living less than wonderful lives. Some people can get no good out of the bad things that happen to them – in fact bad just leads to worse. Is that too awful to bear? Ought we to revert to Platonic or Stoic views that externals really don't matter?

If it's intolerable to say that some people are excluded from the possibility of living good lives, the answer can't be just to retreat from esteeming external goods. The ancient views of the good life are exclusive to the core.

If goods of the soul are all that we really need, it's still true – according to Aristotle *and* Plato *and* the Stoics – that it's partly a matter of luck who has them. Aristotle says it is part of our nature as human beings to grow toward the full development of reason, but he also says some of us are imperfect specimens. Like a stunted rose bush that will never grow tall and bloom abundantly, some of us will not live up to the potential that humans have, collectively, to excel at the use of reason. In his famous argument defending slavery, Aristotle says that some people are natural slaves. They are born without the potential to rule themselves with reason; at best they can obey reason, and so they are better off living under the rule of rational masters. Leaving aside the repugnant notion that less rational people are better off enslaved, we can certainly agree that there are less rational people. The niceties of Aristotelian moral virtue (doing the right thing at the right time to the right person, etc.) are lost on some. These people are also left out of the life of contemplation that Aristotle ranks highest.

Plato also esteems goods of the soul we can't all possess. That resplendent Platonic virtue that trumps all external troubles is a matter of having a soul ruled by reason. It takes a lot of reason to put up with the disadvantages Plato envisions. Plato certainly doesn't think all people have it. It's the philosopher who has it, the person Plato puts in charge of his ideal city in the *Republic*. The other classes that make up this rigidly stratified society do not.

The Stoics tried to spell out and disseminate practical wisdom that could help a person navigate rough waters with equanimity. And many people have found their advice helpful. But could we all be expected to live by that wisdom? We don't all have the mental dexterity it takes to think of our problems in just the way that will make them bearable. The sage who really achieves tranquility in all circumstances is a rarity, as the Stoics admit. Buddhists think the requisite mental discipline is so extraordinary that it's only possible to fully attain it after many rebirths.

Even the gospels, read literally, put our well-being in the hands of a mental achievement that is more accessible to some than to others: the achievement of believing a very hard-to-believe story. A living, breathing, human being, born of an ordinary woman, really was God *and* God's son at the same time, and (though God) died on the cross, but came back to life on the third day, and, through dying, saved us from our sins. For children and the mentally impaired, and even just the literal-minded, understanding this narrative – which presumably must precede believing in its truth – is off limits.

If we do not want to tether the good life to external goods, because that's too exclusive, then we must not tether the good life to goods of the soul either, because that's exclusive as well. Innate luck affects whether we have goods of the soul, like external good fortune affects our external lot in life. But now we have surely gone too far to avoid exclusivity. The ancients may take exclusivity too far – all of them do, whether they're stressing internal goods alone or also external goods. But our deepest conviction is that living a good life does require some measure of luck. That's true when it comes to our internal makeup – our intellectual and emotional health; it's also true when it comes to the external conditions of our lives. When things go wrong, externally, we can find inspiration in Plato and the Stoics, but we find more of the truth – granted, mixed with too much pessimism – in Aristotle.

ARISTOTLE IS PERSUASIVE WHEN he says that reason – ethical and intellectual virtue – is central to living a good life. The core insight, which Aristotle shares with Plato and the Stoics, is that living well and living morally go hand in hand. We will not want to entirely abandon it. Where Aristotle departs from Plato and the Stoics, he's the more convincing. External goods do matter, even if saying so forces us to admit to human vulnerability. I couldn't follow Aristotle on every point. I can't swallow the idea that the good life is identical to the life of full-time philosophers – as much as that view might be flattering to me personally! I'm skeptical of the very idea of *the* good life, if that means a concrete and specific way of life. Even when diluted, so that the idea is that life goes well when, whatever else we do, we approach life rationally, the theory makes us wonder: is reason the only "internal good" that's crucial to good living? If there is a worry that Aristotle's list of critical internal goods might be too short, there's also the concern that his list of critical external goods might be too long or indiscriminate. Must we have money and reasonably good looks; must we even have friends and children? We'll see, as we continue, just how much of Aristotle we really want to retain.

Chapter 4

Is Happiness All That Matters?

Parents have simple wishes for their children, or so it appears when they proclaim that they just want them to be happy. If we weren't sold on reason (or virtue) as the only ingredient of living well, maybe we ought to switch to a different candidate for sole ingredient. Just plain happiness might be what we're looking for.

Plain happiness is nothing as subtle and complex as *eudaimonia*. Happiness, in the plain sense, comprises pleasant states of consciousness (in fact "pleasure" is a virtual synonym): the good feeling of a hot shower, the euphoria of being in love, the sensation of eating chocolate, the pleasant sense of absorption you get from being engrossed in a good book, the pleasure of getting a joke or satisfying curiosity, sexual pleasure, enjoying the coziness of a fire, the pleasure of listening to Mozart, the satisfaction of looking back on a period of your life and judging that things have been going well for you.

Plain happiness fluctuates all the time. You could plot your levels of happiness (and unhappiness) on a graph: think of levels of happiness on the y axis and times on the x axis. A graph of your happiness levels for today might start at the "origin" and move up and to the right along a diagonal path, if you began the day neutrally and steadily became happier and happier. You could use graphs like this to give yourself daily scores for happiness, using the area under the curve to compute your total. An omniscient happiness accountant would be able to give us each one big happiness score at the end of our lives.

Could happiness be the only thing that figures into the assessment of lives, considering that there are so many other things we want, like friends, family, success, and material possessions? Nobody could deny that we place other things on our "wish lists," but the suggestion is that we want the other things for the happiness they generate. Happiness is the only thing that *directly* contributes to the goodness of our lives. If happiness is the only important thing, why is it sometimes reasonable to do things that cause us unhappiness? For the sake of the happiness we anticipate experiencing in the long run. We go to the dentist, take a course in organic chemistry, and the like, because we figure that later on these things will result in greater happiness.

If happiness is the only thing that counts towards making our lives good, it could count in different ways. It could be that only *my* happiness figures into making my life good or bad. The happier I am (and the less unhappy), the better my life is going. On this view we look at a person as a happiness *consumer* when we evaluate his or her life. The alternative is to look at a person both as a consumer and as a *producer* of happiness, and take into account the difference his life makes to the happiness of all people.

Putting it in a nutshell, the view I want to focus on in this chapter champions the lives of the people who are themselves the happiest. We'll call it the "Simple Happiness View." Philosophers call it Hedonism, from the Greek word for pleasure, but that can create confusion, because we ordinarily think of a hedonist as someone who focuses on particularly mindless forms of pleasure; he's the "eat, drink, and be merry" sort of character. A Hedonist, in the philosophical sense, simply says that the sole correct measure of whether a person's life is good or not is the total amount of happiness *that person* experiences over the entire course of his life. A life with more happiness is better than a life with less; the best life is the one with the most happiness.

The talk of measuring is not to be taken too seriously. There isn't really an omniscient happiness accountant. We have gas meters and water meters; we don't have happiness meters. And we don't need them. We have a rough idea of who is especially happy and who is not; which options will bring us more happiness and which less. The question is whether the exclusive focus on amounts of happiness makes sense. Could the truth about the best life be this simple?

BEFORE TRYING TO ANSWER, let's pause to ask whose theory the Simple Happiness View is. Is it actually any philosopher's position?

Epicureanism was a post-Aristotelian rival of Stoicism that identified our final good – our ultimate end – not with virtue but with pleasure. So this is a reasonable first stop on any tour of Simple Happiness View terrain. Though Epicureans value pleasure and pleasure alone, they have some additional distinctive commitments. A day, a week, a year, a life, doesn't go well, they say, when experiences fluctuate from being extremely pleasurable to being extremely painful. To assess a life, it's not just net pleasure (pleasure minus pain) that we need to assess. A graph showing a very flat line above the x axis represents a better life, for the Epicureans, than a bumpy graph depicting higher net pleasure. The Epicureans conceive of a pleasant life as a calm and tranquil life. (If this seems familiar, that is because for the Stoics, too, tranquility, imperturbability, absence of passion, are marks of a good life. Those aren't inherently good ends, for the Stoics – they say only virtue is intrinsically good – but they do picture the good life that way.)

What must we pursue to secure this sort of steadily pleasurable life? A moderate amount of food, alcohol, sex. Plenty of philosophy. An appreciation of the beauties of nature. Aristotle and the Stoics have more admiration for the life of the statesman than the Epicureans do, because the latter see such a life as inevitably full of highs and lows. The most pleasurable life, for the Epicureans, involves retreat: picture spending most of your time sitting in your garden philosophizing with a small group of friends, and you will have a fair idea of the Epicureans' conception of the good life.

Next stop, nineteenth-century England, and the Hedonism embraced by the Utilitarian school of moral philosophy that was developed initially by Jeremy Bentham and then by John Stuart Mill. The Utilitarians did not conceive of the task of moral philosophy in the way the ancients did. For Bentham and Mill, the first question of moral philosophy is not about the life, taken as a whole, that each us should aim to live. The primary moral questions are about the rightness or wrongness of actions. We are making no error if we pluck moral quandaries out of the context of whole lives and try to resolve them. Is it right or wrong to tell a lie? The Utilitarians answer by saying that lying is not intrinsically right or wrong, but right or wrong depending on the consequences in a particular situation. Which it is depends on how much good or bad results from a particular lie, taking into consideration all who are affected, both in the short term and in the long term. But what is good and what is bad? Bentham says the only intrinsic good is pleasure, and the only intrinsic bad is pain. If you add up the pleasure minus the pain for everyone affected by telling a particular lie, you will know whether or not to do it.

Bentham is clear about how to use pleasure and pain to determine rightness and wrongness, but can we also use pleasure and pain to assess how well a life is going? It seems like the only way we could assess a life, if Utilitarianism is correct, would be on the basis of amounts of pleasure and pain, happiness and unhappiness. If happiness is the only intrinsic good, then a life could only be good if the person who lived it "consumed," over time, a great deal of happiness. And that's what the Simple Happiness View says. Could there be any doubt that Utilitarians espouse the Simple Happiness View?

Well, yes. Suppose I love nothing better than to sit by my window watching the world go by while playing tiddlywinks and drinking tea. One day I see a child fall off a bike. Helping the child would interrupt my game of tiddlywinks and leave me with a cold cup of tea. Honestly, it wouldn't give me much pleasure to help. What should I do if I simply want my life to go better? Is my well-being derived from consuming as much pleasure as possible, in which case I should at the very least finish my tea before helping? Or is my well-being derived from doing the right thing, which is to produce as much total pleasure as possible – and get out there as fast as possible? Either answer is consistent with the idea that pleasure is the only intrinsic good.

Unfortunately, Bentham doesn't say. The most significant issue for the ancients, what makes my life good, is not a question in the foreground for him. There's the same indeterminacy in the writing of John Stuart Mill. If I want *my life* to be as good as possible, it's not clear which way he would urge me to go when faced with a choice between maximizing my own pleasure, and maximizing total pleasure. However, there is *some* difference between Mill and Bentham on this score. Bentham thinks it really is possible for someone to enjoy tiddlywinks and tea more than helping an injured child. Pleasure, for different people, comes from different things. For one person, the greatest pleasure will be experienced at the symphony, for another the greatest pleasure will be experienced watching a boxing match. Mill, on the other hand, thinks that the pleasures that involve our higher faculties are qualitatively superior. They really feel better to us, and therefore should count more when we add up pleasures and pains before deciding on a course of action. Among these higher pleasures are the pleasures of doing the right thing. And so

Mill would not be as ready as Bentham to admit that the path that maximizes *my* pleasure could diverge from the path that maximizes *total* pleasure. Rushing to the aid of the child has got to be better both for me and for the child.

Still, even for Mill, there must be some situation that pits the greatest pleasure for me against doing the right thing and producing the greatest total pleasure. Maybe donating to the art museum would give me the greatest pleasure, while donating to the cancer society would generate the most pleasure for all. Which should I choose if I just want *my* life to go best? Would Mill espouse the Simple Happiness View, and identify living well with *consuming* lots of pleasure? Again, the question of the good life is not in the foreground for Mill, as it is for the ancients. He is focused on a different question: what is the right thing to do? Here it's producing happiness that matters, not just consuming it.

The Simple Happiness View is clearly one account of living a good life that Utilitarians could adopt. They could say that while morally we ought to always choose the option that produces the greatest good, our own lives are good or bad depending only on the pleasure we consume, and so sometimes making the morally right choice will involve a sacrifice of our own good. While our actions will be morally right, we will be making our own lives worse. On the other hand, Utilitarians could accept something like the ancient view, which sees virtue as the main ingredient of a good life. They could say that we make our own lives best by always doing the right thing and promoting total happiness, even at our own expense. The more good (happiness) I promote, the better my life is going. The Simple Happiness View seems like the more natural choice for a Utilitarian to make. We saw in the last chapter that it's hard to believe that how well a person's life is going depends entirely or even mainly on moral factors. And that becomes even harder to swallow when we shift from the ancients' conception of morality to the Utilitarians' conception. The Aristotelian virtues are closely linked to emotional stability and mental health, so they have some intuitive relevance to how my life is going. The person who scores high on Utilitarian moral criteria is someone who has a very positive impact on total happiness. Looking at a person's life from that perspective, exclusively, we'll have to ignore a lot of what seems most relevant to the way her life is going.

So much for who espouses the Simple Happiness View. In some moods, *we* do. All in one breath, new parents will say they want their child to have a good life, and they just want the child to be happy. We advise our friends to do things "if it will make you happy." We stop doing things because "it just wasn't making me happy." Happiness is at least a very important part of what we think a good life involves.

A THOUGHT EXPERIMENT DEVISED by contemporary philosopher Robert Nozick helps us examine whether or not happiness is really, ultimately, *all* that matters to us. We will be indulging in a bit of science fiction here. If your literary tastes run in another direction, don't worry: soon we'll return to the real world.

Suppose, Nozick says, there were a device called an "experience machine." The machine controls your brain so that you experience a "virtual world" instead of receiving inputs through your senses from the world around you. If you've seen the movie *The Matrix*, you'll find this easy to visualize. Think of the rebels in the movie reclining in those dentist office type chairs and putting helmets over their heads. The helmets link their brains to a computer that generates a virtual world they call "the matrix." In the movie, the computer is malevolent, but don't think of the experience machine that way. It's run by very kind scientists. The computer in the movie at least partially controls the sort of virtual world that people experience. But the experience machine generates just the virtual world that you would prefer. You get to select the machine's programming before you hook up. If happiness, to you, is climbing mountains, then you can request a virtual world with lots of mountain climbing. If happiness is feeling successful at your job, you can program that into your virtual world. Whatever you want to experience is possible: a loving spouse, charming children, friends who admire you, delicious food that doesn't make you fat. If you find a certain pleasure in contrasts, you can include highs and lows instead of unrelenting good times.

Now, you're not just being given the option to spend the afternoon enjoying some exotic experience. You're going to spend the rest of your life hooked up. (Your bodily needs will be taken care of, so don't worry – but let's not take the time to imagine the details.) This sounds drastic, but you're being offered the possibility of spending the rest of your life in blissful happiness. If you think knowing you are connected to a machine will put a pall on your happiness, the scientists will gladly oblige you by programming the machine to erase your memory of being connected.

Would you sign up? Nozick bets that you wouldn't, and he says that shows that happiness is not really the only thing that matters to you. The disinclination to sign up shows this because connecting to the experience machine would, for most of us, be the way to maximize our happiness. There must be other things we value besides happiness, Nozick concludes – things we could obtain in real life, but not in the experience machine.

Refusal to hook up is not actually so easy to interpret. It could be that we just don't have enough trust in scientists to place ourselves in such a vulnerable position. Maybe they wouldn't comply with our requests. They might want to conduct experiments on us. Or maybe, although the scientists are perfect angels, their machines have the potential to malfunction. Although real life doesn't guarantee us optimal happiness, we might think we're more likely to experience an adequately happy life in the real world.

To eliminate these distractions, let's change the thought experiment a little. The question is not whether you would choose to hook up, but whether you care whether you are right now hooked up. I regret to inform you, but it is just possible that you *did* make the choice to hook up a long time ago. It happened during the experimental days of your adolescence. And yes, you did check the box indicating a preference for memory erasure. So now, of course, you don't remember that fateful day when you lay back in that chair and the helmet was placed over your head. Ever since, you've been living in a virtual world. The friends you thought you had are virtual friends. This book is a virtual book. Your parents are virtual parents. But – now that you think about it – the last several years *have* been exceptionally happy ones! Before you read this, you did think your life was going very well. Do you now have a reason to see things differently?

Nozick predicts you will be discombobulated by these revelations. If you suppose you're hooked up to the experience machine, you will not think that your life is entirely good. I find that many people's thoughts are just what Nozick predicts. They think it would be a bad thing for the life they were living, no matter how happy it is, to be a life generated by an experience machine. There are some people, though, who don't see any problem with such a life. If you're one of them, consider the matter again after thinking a bit about the differences between life "on" the machine and normal life. What are those differences?

To begin with, if we're hooked up to the experience machine, we are dependent on scientists and machines. We are, in some ways, like a patient on life support, whose life can be disrupted, in an instant, by malfunctioning machines or incompetent doctors. In normal life, we enjoy comparative (though of course not absolute) independence.

Hooked up, we do nothing that benefits others. The "care" we take of our virtual children does not benefit anyone, the work we put into curing our virtual patients doesn't cure anyone. The cats we feed are just virtual cats. Our lives don't make a difference. In normal life, we can have a positive impact on others.

"On" the experience machine, we fail in all kinds of ways. Yes, it seems like you got a strike when you went bowling, but you didn't really. You think your daughter got you a lovely father's day present, but that's false. You think you got a raise, but you didn't. If I'm hooked up, nobody ever complies with my demands. I tell my children to do their homework, and although I have an experience which makes it seem like they do, there is no real compliance.

If you're hooked up, you take no risks, you have no real adventures. All that happens to you was planned ahead of time, and guaranteed to go as planned. This could even affect whether you have a chance to develop a real self. When life is entirely planned, you don't have a chance to learn, through trial and error, which activities really suit you, and which don't. In real life, as we grow older, we learn more and more about ourselves through our reactions to the experiences life throws at us.

Clearly, there are differences between ordinary life and life lived through the experience machine. Now that I've brought some to the fore, are you still satisfied with the "hooked-up" life? If you are, that may be because you can't imagine how the alleged problems you'd "suffer" on the experience machine could be problems if they didn't literally cause any suffering. Can there be a problem with my life that doesn't feel like a problem *to me*?

In normal circumstances, our problems typically do feel like problems. But it seems to me that they needn't always. Think of the horror many of us feel at the prospect of winding up in a vegetative state as a result of injury or disease. Many people think this is a worse situation than simply being dead and they prepare living wills in the hope of avoiding being in such a state. My being in a vegetative state is full of problems for others. People would be distraught about me, and my semi-living condition would make it impossible for them to grieve and move on. Maybe as a result of seeing me like that they wouldn't be able to remember me as I used to be. My health care would be tremendously expensive. But aside from all that, it makes sense to think that in a vegetative state I would have problems directly, as well. My condition would be bad *for me*, even though I would have no conscious awareness of that badness.

Dependence, failure to benefit others, having false beliefs – all of these alleged problems on the experience machine wouldn't feel like problems. If I've programmed some altruistic experiences into the experience machine, I'm going to get all the satisfaction from them that I would get in normal life. If I'm not actually benefiting anyone, some would say that that's a problem for others, but not for me. To some, a problem *for me* has got to be a problem affecting my conscious experience. I can understand wanting to use the phrase "for me" that way, but there's this to say on the other side. It's good that I should have a good life – good *for me* in particular, because it's my life. If I'm right now living a bad life, without knowing it, that's bad *for me*, even though the problem may not feel like one.

The idea that there could be problems for me that don't feel like problems has an illustrious supporter – the great French philosopher of the seventeenth century, René Descartes. He was particularly concerned with the problem of having massively false beliefs, which is just one of the problems you would have in the experience machine. Let's consider how that issue arises in Descartes's thinking.

IT'S DESCARTES WHO DESERVES most of the credit for both Nozick's thought experiment and the scenario depicted in *The Matrix*. While Nozick was trying to make a point about values – and maybe the same can be said about *The Matrix* – Descartes's objective was to determine whether there is anything we can know with complete certainty. His ultimate goal was to place science and all knowledge on a secure foundation.

Seventeenth-century guy that Descartes was, he didn't envision being duped by a computer. He asks, in the *Meditations*, whether our conscious experiences could have been directly implanted in us by a nasty, all-powerful being, an Evil Deceiver, instead of coming to us from the world, by way of our sense organs, and our brains. Descartes invites me to see that it's conceivable that there is no physical world out there, and that I have no brain or sense organs. Just conceivably, I could be alone in the universe, but for an Evil Deceiver who's filling my head (no, my soul) with visions of a table, a keyboard, my hands on the keyboard, the computer screen, the window, the trees beyond the window, the sky. All those things could be illusory.

After Descartes admits that his beliefs could be massively false, he discovers, to his delight, that there is one thing he can't doubt, and that's the bare fact of his existence. "I think, therefore I am," he insists. This famous sentence has the air of telling us something deep about the meaning of life, but to Descartes it expresses the simplest possible certainty. If I'm thinking about whether I exist, how could I possibly *not* exist? OK, he says, I exist, but what else can I be sure of? Descartes proceeds, baby-step by baby-step, trying to discover additional certainties. Using a combination of reasonably robust first principles and not-so-evident principles, he arrives at the conclusion that there is a God who is perfectly good. This is just as certain, he claims, as the proposition that I exist. Well, maybe. What's relevant for us is the next step. I have the strongest possible inclination to believe that there is a desk in front of me; there's nothing I can do to stifle that inclination for good (well . . . maybe for a few minutes, but inevitably the belief returns). If there's really no desk there, then God would have to be guilty of either deceiving me or allowing me to be deceived by another power. But deception is bad, Descartes assumes. God is good. He wouldn't deceive me *or* allow me to be deceived! So there must actually *be* a desk in front of me.

We have to pause here to note the amazing centrality this reasoning gives to our religious beliefs. If Descartes is right, I have to *first* know that God exists before I can know this desk exists (or my body, even). And an atheist is just out of luck. He *can't* have any rational basis for believing that the desk exists!

The relevant thing is Descartes's assumption that it would be a very bad thing for me to have loads of beliefs that are completely out of whack with reality. It's not a matter of causing me any conscious problem. It's just a bad thing, period. It's not something a perfectly good being would impose on me. This part of the argument seems to me to be very strong. A person whose entire understanding of the world around her is massively incorrect does have a problem, whether or not to her it feels like one. And that bears on what we say about people attached to the experience machine and people in vegetative states. It's a problem for them to be in those states, even though the problem does not take a conscious form. You can have a problem, without being aware of it.

Question for *Matrix* fans: Do the characters in the movie see sheer deception as a problem? I think they do, but their motivations are complex. The rebels exit virtual reality and stay in the real world partly because they want to avoid being deceived, but also because that's the only way to stop the evil computer from taking over the world. It's not *just* the badness of unconscious deception that motivates them. And then there are characters willing to return to virtual reality, with memory erasure, despite knowing they will wind up completely deceived. This doesn't show they don't find deception problematic. Reality has turned out to be ugly and miserable, and the virtual world of "the Matrix" is reasonably pleasant. It's fair to say that those who return do see being deceived as evil; they just see it as the lesser evil, compared to non-stop reality-based unhappiness. And so the movie's characters don't behave in a way that conflicts with my point: being massively deceived is a problem for me whether or not it feels like one. Good and bad things for me are not always things that feel good to me or feel bad to me.

IF I'VE MADE MY case so far, then the door is now open to saying there are good things besides happiness, and bad things besides unhappiness. I think we ought to walk through that door. Happiness really isn't all that matters. Imagine your own child growing up and reading about the experience machine in a magazine. She decides that this is her goal in life and begins to spend all of her time planning what kinds of programming she will request. You would certainly have ample reason to object. There are the worries about whether she will be safe. Equally, you're going to be aghast at the prospect of your child being "dead" to you. You will not be soothed much by her reassurances that she will have you programmed in as a denizen of her virtual world. But beyond all of that, I think you're probably going to be disappointed by the life your daughter plans to live. This is not at all what you wanted for her. There is something fundamentally bad about that life, even if the badness will never be felt by your daughter.

We've mulled over various candidates for the nature of that badness. There are the problems of dependence, of being deceived, of doing nothing for others. But there are more. Aristotle would complain that life hooked up is an unnatural life. You might complain that it's a life in which body-based talents like piano playing and swimming and cooking can't be developed. It's also a life that makes no contribution to knowledge or culture. On the other hand, the goodness that's available in the experience machine may not be exclusively the goodness of being happy. Possibly intelligence and good character are available and they may contribute directly to the goodness of our lives, not just indirectly, by making us happier. The list of things that might be good besides happiness, and bad besides unhappiness, grows longer and longer.

Once we start thinking that happiness is all that matters, that idea has a grip on us that's difficult to loosen. I've tried to loosen it by throwing out a wide variety of apparent good things and bad things, but they won't all be retained. In the next chapter, I start a more systematic inventory of what really ought to be considered essential to a good life.

But let's pause before moving in that direction. Like the bad guy at the end of the horror movie, let's let the single-factor view of a good life have one final rampage. Why not say that our lives go well just so long as we get what we want, whatever that may be? The person whose every desire is fulfilled lives a great life, and the person whose desires are constantly frustrated lives an awful life. At the end of the nineteenth century, the American philosopher William James championed this idea in its baldest conceivable form: *"[T]he essence of good is simply to satisfy demand. The demand may be for anything under the sun."*

The desire-fulfillment theory (as it's sometimes called) sounds identical to relativism, but it isn't, exactly. The desire-fulfillment theory takes a stand on what matters. Relativism takes no stand. It pays equal respect to the view that desire-fulfillment is good, if that's what some individual or culture says; and to the view that the frustration of desires is good, if that's what some individual or culture says. And some cultures actually do. As we saw in Chapter 2, it seems as if the culture of the desert saints valued the frustration of desires. Our lives go best, they thought, the *less* that our physical desires are fulfilled. A proponent of the desire-fulfillment theory could not go along with that.

The desire-fulfillment theory also sounds a lot like the Simple Happiness Theory. After all, usually when we get what we want, we feel happy, and when we don't get what we want, we feel unhappy. But again, these two views are not exactly the same. Think of a happy son who is hooked up to the experience machine. If his desire is to be a reliable son, and his real mother is on her deathbed (with him nowhere in sight), then the verdict of the desire-fulfillment view is that his life isn't going so well. The Simple Happiness View says his life is going great, so long as he's happy.

The basic idea of the desire-fulfillment theory is attractive: the idea is to connect what's good for you with what *you* want. The view demands neutrality toward what you happen to want, thereby respecting *you* as a fashioner of your own desires, values, and choices; on the other hand, it honors the fulfillment of your desires, values, and choices as a good thing. By all appearances, this is an idea that's admirably egalitarian. It's an idea that seems to comport well with valuing and honoring individual autonomy.

But does it really? The trouble is that it's only in an ideal world that people are truly fashioners of their own desires, values, and choices. Many of our desires are the result of manipulation, misinformation, or downright deception. We want the things we are encouraged to want by commercials and billboards. After seeing enough commercials for the latest, greatest new car, you might find yourself wanting one very badly; if we say it's good for your life if you succeed in getting yourself one, are we really honoring *you* as fashioner of your own desires, or are we honoring some Madison Avenue advertising firm?

Maybe you can disentangle what you really, truly, deeply want from your more casual material longings, and maybe the desire-fulfillment theory might make a distinction so that there's more good in the fulfill-ment of the former. The problem is that in many cases there is no clear line. A 16-year-old girl can ardently wish to be the tenth wife of an elderly Mormon patriarch. And he might cite her wants as justification for going ahead with the marriage. But if he says her life will go better if she marries him, we know he's not honoring her as a shaper of her own life. Her desires have been ingeniously manipulated by a multitude of means so that the patriarch can use them as an excuse to fulfill his own.

Even where there is no clear-cut manipulating going on, a person's desires can be shaped by circumstances so drastically that respecting the desires is really just acceding to the circumstances. In *Women and Human Development*, contemporary philosopher Martha Nussbaum describes the "adaptive preferences" of women in traditional societies who acquiesce in their own discrimination. Sometimes it's easier to col-laborate than go through life feeling angry and aggrieved. For example, she speaks of an Indian woman who happily does all the housework, even though she does grueling work outside the home and her husband barely works at all.

Because of these worries, proponents of the desire-fulfillment theory tend to decorate the theory with all sorts of carefully crafted qualifications. It's not any desire that ought to be fulfilled, but only the desires that are formed in the right way. These first-class desires are formed freely and rationally. Proponents have to define "freely" and "rationally" carefully, so that they don't abandon the neutrality of the theory. They can't allow themselves to think that rational desires are aimed at some set of intrinsically good things, because they don't want to be committed to any such thing.

Many contemporary philosophers have views that, on close inspection, are forms of the desire-fulfillment theory. For example, the dominant form of Utilitarianism today identifies the good we should be trying to maximize not with pleasure or happiness, but with the satisfaction of preferences, or (sometimes) *rational* preferences; a satisfied preference is much the same as a fulfilled desire. One of the most influential political philosophers of our time, John Rawls, defines what's good for an individual as the fulfillment of a rational life plan. A life plan is something you establish early in life that encompasses the key things you want, and how you will try to obtain them. A person who fulfills his life plan will have fulfilled many of his key desires, so Rawls's account of what's good for an individual is a variation on the desire-fulfillment theme. Your life plan is rational if it doesn't involve errors of logic and you make your plan "with full awareness of the relevant facts, and after a careful consideration of the consequences."

It's a popular theory with undeniable appeal, but even with careful tinkering, the desire-fulfillment theory runs into problems. What if you have no life plan, or you even have an irrational life plan? Suppose, for example, your plan is to establish a career in your twenties and thirties, and then have children around the age of 40 (when fertility in women precipitously declines), though motherhood is critically important to you. An irrational life plan! But if it succeeds, isn't that cause for celebration? It seems clear that a life can go well despite the fact that it *doesn't* fulfill any rational desire or plan.

And on the other hand, sometimes a life does not go well even though it does fulfill a rational desire or plan. Here's a case of a person with well-informed, non-manipulated, deep and stable desires for his own life that have come to be thoroughly fulfilled. The man's name is Shridhar

Chillal, and he lives in Poona, India. I would know nothing about him except that he's in the *Guinness Book of World Records* because he has the longest fingernails in the world – 20 feet worth on one hand. The weight has caused permanent nerve damage on that side of his body, resulting in permanent deafness; his nails stop him from engaging in normal activities or even getting a good night's sleep. Illogical? Irrational? He made his plan with full information and has what he wants most: the longest fingernails, fame. He thinks the disabilities are a reasonable price to pay for his success and has no regrets.

The desire-fulfillment theory, however we tinker with it, would have to recognize Shridhar Chillal's life as a great one. That makes me uncomfortable with the desire-fulfillment theory. Undeniably, there's some importance in getting what we want. In none of the examples that I've discussed can we entirely dismiss actual wants. But it does seem like there's more that ought to be considered when we take stock of whether someone has led a good life or not. Certainly, we are not prepared to pronounce a life a failure, solely on grounds that a person did *not* get what he most wanted. In fact, great lives seem to be able to encompass great disappointments. The paraplegic does not walk again, the author doesn't get the fame he wants, the political activist doesn't get his candidate elected – if the desire-fulfillment theory were correct, these kinds of failures would be absolutely pivotal to our assessment of lives. They are not nothing, but they are not as central as the desire-fulfillment theory would have it.

The appeal of the desire-fulfillment theory should not be forgotten as we begin to fashion a new account of what it is to live well in the next chapter. We need to grant some importance to desire-fulfillment. But getting what you want is no more plausible than virtue or happiness as the *sole* factor affecting whether or not our lives go well.

Chapter 5

Necessities

There's something marvelous about the very idea that just one thing matters in life. It would be amazing if it were true, and in a way wonderful. Think how much easier it would be to make decisions and plans if there were only one thing ultimately worth having. This is an enticement for philosophers who prefer to think of what's ultimately valuable as something singular.

There would be advantages if there were just one form of good, but life would be a bit dull. A popular story line traces the journey from bad to good, or at least worse to better. Stories of improvement are as diverse as *Crime and Punishment*, nineteenth-century slave memoirs, and the biography of Helen Keller. On any one-value view, all these worse-to-better stories must tell essentially the same tale. If they really do plot life improvement, then they must all be stories of somebody getting happier, or becoming more virtuous, or becoming more . . . whatever.

The truth is certainly more interesting. The trajectories of improvement are varied. But are they infinitely varied? That might be especially interesting, but it would also be bewildering. For every story of a life getting better, there's someone who had to live that life "from the inside." He or she had to settle on aims, sometimes letting go of one thing to pursue another. If an unlimited number of valuable things demanded attention, our heads would spin. We should at least prefer to find that there is some manageable core to what's worth pursuing.

We get an implicit sense of the various things that have worth by immersing ourselves in life stories. That implicit sense is probably more satisfying than any tidy, explicit list could be. But our job here is to make things clear and precise. So the goal is in fact a list. I'll try to keep some flesh on the bones of this enterprise by returning as often as can be to the stories themselves. They will be a part of our evidence for what belongs on the list.

The things we want on our list are fundamentally good – good in their own right, not because of anything else. Many stories of life getting better relate to how food and shelter were obtained, or health was restored, or safety was secured. These can be really good stories. (My favorite of this kind is Steven Callahan's *Adrift*, which recounts the 72 days he spent alone in a lifeboat.) When we're in the midst of these kinds of struggles, nothing is so intensely important to us as being fed, getting warm, being free of pain and disease, or getting out of the way of danger. But really, health and safety don't seem good purely for themselves, but because of all the things that are possible when we have them. A story of recovery from an illness, if it ends with simple health, isn't always a story with a conclusive ending. The person who has recovered is in a better position to have a life that goes well. But he may or may not actually have one.

There's no reason to think that every fundamental good makes a difference to how our lives go. It's conceivable that there are ultimate goods that don't play a direct role in our lives. For example, you might think that ecosystems are better or worse off depending on how diverse they are. Biological diversity, on this view, is an ultimate good. But this particular ultimate good (if it is one) doesn't have much to do with an individual life. It obviously shouldn't be placed on the list we're after. And then, it's possible that there are fundamental goods that could make a life go better, but not a human life. Perhaps omniscience would make the life of a supreme being as good as it can be, but it wouldn't be beneficial for us (would it be good if you knew what your spouse was thinking all the time?). There might be fundamental goods that make animal lives go better, but not ours.

The fundamental goods we want to focus on are *relevant* to a human life. But relevant how? As long as we were envisaging just one good, like happiness, the idea of relevance was clear-cut. That good had to be understood as being necessary to making a life go well. Having enough of that good had to be sufficient to make a life go well. Even if there are merely two fundamental goods, X and Y, a new question emerges. Does a life get to be overall good just from being imbued with a lot of X *or* Y, in whatever proportion, or must both X *and* Y be present? On the first alternative, X and Y are interchangeable. Lots of one can make up for little of the other. On the second, they both deliver good, but they deliver it in importantly different, non-interchangeable forms. Each is a necessity. To complicate matters, the truth could be mixed. Different fundamental goods could be relevant in different ways. Some could be necessities, comprising a sort of "A" list, and others interchangeable contributors, making it only onto a "B" list.

If there are fundamental goods that are necessities, they would play a special role in our lives. We would have to reserve some of our energy for obtaining them, and pay special attention to them in thinking about the way we raise and teach our children, and how our societies are structured. Since necessities would play such a special role in our lives, we'll be particularly focused on identifying fundamental goods with this status – the items on the "A" list.

What kind of evidence would show that something is a fundamental good that's not just relevant to living well, but necessary? There certainly isn't anything like a sure-fire test. We can only aspire to say what seems most reasonable. We certainly should not expect to be able to recognize which are the critical goods in one intuitive flash, without spending time looking at any sort of evidence. It may take you some time before you come to think that happiness or morality, or any other candidate, is fundamentally good. A person could come to think so only after reading a searing biography, or watching a movie, or reflecting on a life experience. At the very least, you would have to sift through examples. We're all familiar with lots of lives and we deem some better than others. If the lives we deem good consistently are lives of – say – eating lots of popcorn, then eating lots of popcorn looks to be a fundamental good with relevance to human well-being. If we deem lives bad when they're lacking popcorn consumption, then that's a reason to view popcorn consumption as a necessity.

Beyond this sort of sifting of cases and discovery of patterns, we learn something from looking at human motivation. Since I'm no more astute a judge of value than anyone else, it pays to think about what people value and how they value it. If many people will stop at nothing to procure popcorn, that's some support for regarding eating popcorn as a necessity. That's not to say that we need to do surveys to show that everyone wants popcorn. The occasional popcorn hater doesn't refute the theory that it's necessary, because, as I said at the end of the previous chapter, desires are manipulable; they're not definitive. But they're certainly a piece of relevant evidence.

Finally, it's got to help to get to the bottom of the talk of necessities. What (on earth!) could make any fundamental good a necessity, instead of merely one optional way to add goodness to a life? Once you know the basis of this kind of necessity, that would surely help you determine what's necessary and what's not.

In this chapter and the next, all these considerations will play some role. Here I will be particularly concerned with cases and patterns and motivations. The basis for necessity is going to come up in the next chapter.

HAPPINESS IS A REASONABLE place to begin. Some philosophers have questioned whether feelings of happiness are good at all, let alone fundamentally good. The Stoics, for example, argue that plain physical pleasure adds nothing positive at all to a life that is good because of virtue:

> It is like the light of a lamp eclipsed and obliterated by the rays of the sun; like a drop of honey lost in the vastness of the Aegean sea; a penny added to the riches of Croesus, or a single step on the road from here to India. Such is the value of bodily goods that it is unavoidably eclipsed, overwhelmed and destroyed by the splendour and grandeur of virtue . . .

Kant takes a kindred stand when he says that the only thing that's good without qualification is the morally good will. If feeling happy is sometimes good, and perhaps even for itself, it's not good at those times when it's enticing us in the wrong direction or rewarding evil deeds.

My intuitions side with the Hedonistic Utilitarians of the last chapter. Happiness is a good thing, always. We don't like to see bad people experience happiness precisely because we do think it's something good, and we want them to have no share of what's good. There's something disturbing about ill-gotten happiness. It's especially creepy to contemplate sadistic pleasure, pleasure that's actually derived from causing others to suffer. But I don't think we can assess whether five minutes of happiness is good or not based on its pedigree. Happiness is good, period.

And it's relevant to how well a life is going. In *Darkness Visible*, William Styron tells the story of a depression that overwhelmed him and nearly drove him to suicide; as the depression lifts, and he has his first moments of non-misery, and then moments of happiness, there's no doubt that his life is going better. You could insist that greater happiness was life-enhancing for him because it paid off in greater creativity or healthier relationships, or some other coin, but that's not what seems to be the case. Think of a time when your own life was not going well. Gradually, you started to be happier. You found your days more pleasant. You enjoyed the company of your friends more. Your boss didn't annoy you as much. You weren't dwelling on worries about the future any more. This change of mood probably improved your life – directly, and because of itself. Happiness, whether it comes about in mysterious ways, in good ways, or in bad ways, is a fundamental good that can directly affect how our lives are going.

If happiness is relevant to the way a life is going, is it also necessary? Without at least some happiness, it does not seem like we can reach the level of even minimally good lives. A person without any happiness at all is unconscious, or continually miserable, or at best in a neutral frame of mind. Of these possibilities, neutrality certainly seems the most appealing, but it's hard to imagine a person constantly in such a state whose life could be judged positively, overall.

HAPPINESS IS CRITICAL, BUT it's not the only critical thing. David Shipler portrays the lives of people struggling to make ends meet in his recent book, *The Working Poor: Invisible in America*. His stories have a recurrent theme: the lack of control that's the cost of poverty. The low-income workers he portrays are deprived of independence, autonomy, self-determination. They have no chance to be the authors of their own lives.

One of his portraits is particularly touching. Caroline works in the women's department at Wal-Mart. She needs to be home with her teen-aged daughter in the evenings, because of her mental retardation and epilepsy, but she's forced to work night shifts. She'd have better hours and make better money as a manager, but – perhaps because she's missing all her teeth – she's repeatedly passed over for promotion. She finally quits the Wal-Mart job, and then one business after another gives her irregular night shifts, until her daughter's teachers become concerned that she's being neglected. Caroline finally loses both her home and her daughter, who goes to live with a relative.

Nobody has perfect control. But there is a level of autonomy beneath which we do not want to fall. Barbara Ehrenreich, in *Nickel and Dimed*, describes the way control is lost even before a person is hired. The job applicant has to take drug tests and fill out phony psychological question-naires. If hired, the blue-collar worker finds herself being told exactly how every aspect of the job must be performed. In the worst cases, the worker becomes little more than a cog in a machine. Shipler describes a woman in Los Angeles sewing flies into blue jeans at a rate of 767 per hour, on pain of being docked a portion of her hourly wage of $5.75. In the very worst cases, the worker is physically prevented from escaping her thing-like status; she is nearly a slave.

Having more control is one thing, it seems, that would have made Caroline's life better. It would have been a major improvement if she could have controlled her work schedule to accommodate her daughter's needs. Advancing to a managerial position would have increased her control over her daily activities. It would have been some improvement if she had been given the chance to initiate and innovate on the job, instead of having to follow rigidly prescribed routines.

Is autonomy really something we should value in itself? For Aristotle it is all too obvious that a slave has no chance of living a good life. Still, a natural slave, a person deficient in reason, ought to remain a slave. When irrational people are put in charge of themselves, reason does not have a chance to rule, and that's the worst situation of all. What's valu-able, to Aristotle, is *rational* autonomy, not mere autonomy. What if the exercise of autonomy leads Caroline to reorganize the women's clothing department by color (all the green clothes here, all the purple clothes there); or spend most of her salary on lottery tickets; what if she lost her teeth by choosing to eat candy all day? Is self-determination valuable regardless of its outcome?

What I'll say about foolish exercises of autonomy is just what I said about ill-gotten happiness. Autonomy is always, as such, good. What would be *too* counterintuitive would be to say that every increase in autonomy automatically makes a person's life overall better. But we needn't say that. There are other things a life needs besides autonomy, and foolish exercises of autonomy will typically get in the way of the fulfillment of those other needs.

Lack of autonomy tends to be accompanied by unhappiness and greater autonomy by greater happiness. It's difficult, therefore, to disen-tangle the desire to be more autonomous from the desire to be happier. Still, unless we are utterly determined to construe happiness as the sole motivator in life, the pursuit of autonomy is everywhere to see: it's evident when slaves demand freedom from masters, when teenagers demand more independence from parents, when workers wrestle some control over their hours from managers, when women demand the right to vote.

In contemporary Western culture, there's no doubt that we place a huge premium on personal autonomy. Autonomy is regarded in quite a different way in other settings. Certainly we should avoid drawing a picture of the necessary kinds and amounts of autonomy based on what's in our own backyards. Arranged marriage is alien to us, but does it cut into autonomy excessively? An Indian couple I know tell me how their marriage was arranged in their twenties by thoughtful parents looking out for their best interests; their marriage seems as good as most. On the other hand, in traditional Hindu villages, it's not unusual for parents to arrange the marriage of a girl as young as eight, who is then kept behind the walls of her home until she's old enough to join her husband's household. In this case, unlike the first, there's a disturbing loss of control. In saying so, we're not necessarily holding an alien idea about individual lives over the local one. The local assumption seems really to be that the girl is just a girl, and not entitled to the best life – an idea we are compelled to reject. Her individual interests are regarded as subordinate to the interests of men, or families, or the village as a whole.

Insisting that a good life includes "enough" autonomy seems to particularly conflict with the most traditional Islamic ideas about the good life for women, but again, the contradiction can be read in another way. In Saudi Arabia, women live out their lives in *purdah* hidden in their fathers' or husbands' homes, and behind veils. They depend on male relatives to take them places and are denied the right to vote. As Martha Nussbaum points out in *Women and Human Development*, it's not necessarily true that social arrangements reveal a vision of the best life for a woman; arrangements are often defended because they're thought to be best for society as a whole. The good for individual women doesn't count, or counts for less. By contrast, she supports – persuasively – "a principle of each person as an end."

Surely, though, there are cultures quite unlike our own that really do conceive of what it is for an individual to live well in ways that give less emphasis to autonomy. In Thomas à Kempis's fifteenth-century classic, *The Imitation of Christ*, the advice to the devout is to find someone to obey. Letting someone else run your life is regarded as good, not bad (as long as you attach yourself to the right superior). The ideal of limiting oneself is taken about as far as possible in some of the medieval religious orders. In *Galileo's Daughter*, Dava Sobel describes the religious order where Galileo – that highly disobedient Catholic – sent his own daughters. In the order of Saint Clare, life was spent within the confines of a convent. The confinement was supposed to facilitate a virtuous life. So Saint Colette explains:

> He Himself deigned and willed to be placed in a sepulchre of stone. And it pleased Him to be so entombed for forty hours. So, my dear Sisters, you follow Him. For after obedience, poverty, and pure chastity, you have holy enclosure to hold on to, enclosure in which you can live for forty years either more or less, and in which you will die.

Imprisonment in the convent was taken to be a good life for the individual sisters, not just a means to some greater collective good.

Stretch our preconceptions as we may, we have to be prepared to say that some views are just wrong. The idea that loss of autonomy is conducive to living the best life is a view that has been superseded by other ideas, even within the monastic tradition, and rightly so.

HAPPINESS, AUTONOMY. COULD THOSE be all the necessities there are? "Nowhere Man" must give us pause. He is well endowed with both, but his name is based on the fact that one week he's working at a slaughterhouse, but the next week he quits and works at the local animal shelter. Now he's actively involved in Republican politics. Next he's earnestly supporting the Democratic Party. He gets excited about Buddhism and then he's moved on to Jewish Mysticism. "Doesn't have a point of view, knows not where he's going to," as the Beatles song so aptly puts it.

Nowhere Man's problem, on the surface, is that there is no unity or continuity in his life. That sounds like a merely aesthetic criticism (this novel is choppy; it doesn't hang together; the midsection doesn't belong). It seems too abstract to really be relevant to evaluating a life; until, that is, we reframe the problem as a lack of self. We want to be amply endowed with the ingredients covered so far (happiness and autonomy), but we want our way of pursuing them to spring from our "selves."

If we really have a grip on Nowhere Man's problem, we ought to be able to identify instances of it in the real world, and that is harder than one might expect. People's lives can exhibit considerable contrast and variety without anyone suspecting a missing "self." There's no problem with Arnold Schwarzenegger's life, just because he went from action hero in the movies to California governor, or because he's a Republican married into the famously Democratic Kennedy family. It's not the sheer disunity of a life that's bad, but an underlying weak self, a self without any strong preferences. A weak self is indifferent to what, for the rest of us, are big differences. No steady convictions and personal traits control perceptions of what's appealing and what's not. Beyond that, it's hard to say what a strong self is, exactly. But it seems critical to our lives going well. If being autonomous and self-determining are as important as they seem to be, it must be equally important for a person to have a self that does the determining.

A sense of identity tends to make us happy, like the other fundamental goods do. But self and happiness don't always go hand in hand. There's probably some situation in which each of us would choose self over happiness. Some people face that choice as the result of a mental illness. For a person who is profoundly depressed, a treatment of last resort is electroconvulsive therapy, which can result in memory loss. With whole swaths of one's life erased – who your friends were, what you read or wrote, where you traveled, what happened in the world at large – you can become virtually another person. Jonathan Cott reports just this in his memoir *On the Sea of Memory*; he seems to lament having chosen ECT to treat severe depression, longing for a return of self, even a self that was depressed. In *Listening to Prozac*, Peter Kramer worries that the alteration of identity is a quite standard effect of anti-depressants, and wonders whether mood improvement is worth the cost.

Injury to self can be done by medications and memory loss, but the causes are innumerable. Shipler's book sheds light on one of the many ways that people stuck in poverty sometimes come to have problems of "self." Many are victims of sexual abuse who suffer dissociative disorders. In other words, they split off a part of themselves and become mere observers of the abuse. This spares them some of the pain of their victimization, but later they continue to observe as things "happen" to them. They watch themselves neglecting their own children instead of choosing to neglect them or choosing to stop neglecting them.

But problems of self are not just outcomes of poverty. To cite just one literary example, in Zora Neale Hurston's *Their Eyes Were Watching God*, Janie's first two marriages are to well-off men who define the social role she is supposed to play. The way they use her to adorn themselves stops her from finding her own voice. Descending to a lower socio-economic stratum, ironically, she discovers a sense of self. Shipler describes how rich parents neglect children and bestow on them an insidious hunger for attention. They become anxious "people pleasers." A child like this reaches adulthood with a set of traits, interests, and abilities that win Mom and Dad's approval. The adult child winds up with no deep-rooted self at the helm. She casts about, now doing this, now doing that. Even if the thises and thats are good things and produce some happiness, there seems to be something amiss with such a life.

Like autonomy, self-expression is especially prized in contemporary Western societies. But is self merely a Western preoccupation? On the face of it, Buddhist thinking involves a diametrically opposed sense of value. Buddhist sages urge us to lose ourselves, not find ourselves; the very highest thing we can achieve is "no self." The phrase is deliberately enigmatic and there is no end of literature about what it means. Vietnamese monk Thich Nhat Hanh cautions his readers to interpret the *dharma*, the teachings of the Buddha, with an awareness of the relevant audience. When the Buddha taught no-self, he was speaking to Vedic priests of ancient India, who used the notion of *atman* to justify "the social injustice of the day – the caste system, the terrible treatment of the untouchables, and the monopolization of spiritual teachings by those who enjoyed the best material conditions and yet were hardly spiritual at all. In reaction, the Buddha emphasized the teachings of non-Atman (non-self)." What I am putting forward as a necessity has nothing to do with an immaterial soul or an inborn fixed essence. It's being your own person, knowing yourself, being true to yourself, having your own center; *not* merely imitating, blending in, or bouncing around mindlessly from one thing to the next.

Though Buddhism encourages the realization of no-self, it doesn't encourage us to be like Nowhere Man. I'm inclined to think a Buddhist *doesn't* reject self as I am using the term. What no-self really means is not being rigidly identified with some narrow set of characteristics (I am a female liberal intellectual), not being focused on acquisition, not being egocentric. It is being open, receptive, compassionate.

It's certainly true that if we were to define what self-expression amounts to on the basis of Western models, we would fail to stretch far enough beyond our own cultural frontiers. The self-expression of an Andy Warhol is one thing. But self-expression is not the exclusive preserve of the flamboyant, rebellious, and self-centered. It's also self-expression to plant a garden in your own way, to devise your own versions of family recipes, to simply have your own point of view.

MORALITY WAS ONE OF the goods that was missing for the person hooked up to the experience machine (Chapter 4). The person who is hooked up puts his energy into phantom moral responsibilities and neglects real ones. Perhaps his virtual mother decides to learn Italian and he generously buys her audiotapes and takes her to Rome. Meanwhile, his real mother is lying in the hospital and her long-lost son never so much as visits. My intuition is that this person's life is not going as well as he thinks it is. His moral failings stop him from being able to live even a basically good life.

Morality pertains to the way we treat others, most prominently, but also concerns the way we treat ourselves. It's a moral problem if you permit others to exploit you, or you do nothing to avoid terrible health. That the self-regarding portion of morality should make a difference in a person's life is not so surprising. What's more perplexing is the suggestion that all of morality, the self-regarding and the other-regarding aspects, make a positive difference to individual well-being.

My intuitions about the critical role of morality agree with the ancients – Plato, Aristotle, and the Stoics – who all regard moral virtue as central to living our lives well. For some of the ancients, the benefit of morality is so significant that morality is the only thing that determines how my life is going. I can't swallow that whole, but morality can, intuitively, make me a better person and my life a better life. It's not always a matter of morality making me happy – though frequently it does. Morality seems to make a direct difference to how well my life is going.

Certainly, there are stories of life getting better because of moral improvement. In Dostoevsky's *Crime and Punishment*, Raskolnikov kills an old woman, struggles to justify himself to himself and his friends, but eventually feels compelled to take responsibility. At the end of the book, he walks up the steps of the police station and confesses, with no particular sensation of pleasure or pain. We know his life is now going better, even before we read the epilogue and find out what happens to him. It's true that his confession has rewards: he's given a lenient sentence because he's admitted to his crime; he's now able to enjoy and reciprocate the love of the devoted and saintly Sonya; and he winds up turning tentatively in the direction of her religious faith. Moments of "infinite happiness" arrive while Raskolnikov serves his term in a Siberian prison camp, and more are assured in the future. But the moment when his life has become better precedes the happiness payoff. The sheer moral improvement at the moment of his confession establishes some life improvement before greater happiness comes along and yields more.

The scope and nature of morality are deeply puzzling. Still, the idea that morality is a requirement is not vacuous. We all share at least a sketchy, intuitive idea about which kinds of endeavors have moral merit – doing a favor for an ailing neighbor, keeping a promise to a friend, avoiding roads that lead to addiction or prostitution. And we have a rough idea of the endeavors that have a sort of merit that's non-moral – climbing a mountain, making a delicious meal, reading Russian novels. Do we adhere to the demands of morality by having the right character – by being courageous and truthful and wise, and the rest – as Aristotle and the Stoics think? Is morality a matter of doing the right thing, possibly by promoting the greatest possible happiness for all, as the Utilitarians think? There are these and many other ways of explicating what morality amounts to. Depending on how morality is understood, it can be easier or harder to see the connection between being moral and living well.

The ancient conceptions, with their focus on virtue, are most conducive to seeing the connection. As we saw in Chapter 3, the Aristotelian virtues are sustainers of stability and balance. Being angry at the right time, at the right person, to the right degree, would save a person from being a doormat or a volcano. It's harder to say why a person can make his life go better by sending money to help flood victims on the other side of the world, or by telling the truth in an awkward situation, or by apportioning grades or pay increases fairly. What's the relevance of doing these things for other people to making your own life go well?

Perhaps it comes down to a connection between living well and living among others. If you concern yourself not at all with what you owe to others or with what they need from you, you live in profound isolation. Yes, there are people out there, but in your scheme of things, they're just things – like the rocks in a quarry or the cornstalks in a field. Without morality, you would enjoy, protect, exploit, or destroy others at your pleasure. You would regard yourself as the only one of your kind, the only one whose well-being really matters. If it would be bad to literally be the only one of your kind, the last surviving person, then it's bad to live as if you were. The good of moral behavior toward others, for each of us, is the good of being part of a richer world, in which there are many beings with independent importance.

Morality is good for us because it makes us less alone – it gives me a kind of friendship not just with my *friends* but with everyone. If friendship strikes you as an obvious good, then this explanation will satisfy you. But what if it doesn't? There is this also to say: there is something painfully limited about our lives. You can only live one life – here, not there; now, not in the past or the future; doing this, not that. We break through these limits by identifying with hungry people on the other side of the globe or with the inhabitants of a polluted, over-heated world in the next century. We become (a bit) *them*. Ethical concern is something of a cure for our sense of finitude. It's good to do the right thing because it gives you an expanded life, one that encompasses not just your own feelings and satisfactions and accomplishments, but those of other people (and possibly animals as well).

Though rather abstract, these thoughts might sustain us through some of our moral travails. Yes, I *will* make a donation to Oxfam, because it is a good thing to be tied by invisible threads to people around the world. Yes, I'll buy a hybrid car, because I identify with the people in the next century who are in danger of living in a drastically altered, warm and watery world. No, I won't make my life easier by giving all my students high grades, because it's really not good for them, or for anyone else, and I recognize everyone's welfare as being just as important as my own.

Such thoughts will often shepherd us toward the right resolution of our quandaries, but not always. Keeping promises, paying the taxes you owe, speaking the truth, giving fair grades, sacrificing for others – all these things can cost a lot. I think they do always add some good to a person's life, but in some situations doing the right thing drives out other good things. Morality can be like the squash and pumpkin plants that are right now starting to engulf my garden. I added a plus to the garden by planting them, but pretty soon there aren't going to be any carrots. Morality isn't the magic ingredient that always makes a life go better on the whole. Still, it is a life enhancer as far as it goes, and so critical as to count as a necessity. (Should you always do the right thing, even when morality encroaches on the other necessities, and you don't stand to benefit? We'll come to that difficult question in Chapter 8.)

A LIST OF FOUR necessities – happiness, autonomy, self-expression, and morality – is admirably tidy, but not absurdly restrictive. Each thing on the list is robustly valuable. We certainly act like these things are critically important in our daily lives. Now we enter less certain territory.

Take, to begin with, a woman I will call Constance. She works as a piano teacher, plays Beethoven sonatas splendidly, enjoys going to the symphony. She wears attractive, timeless fashions picked out of the Land's End catalogue and reads the Bible in her spare time. She's a good friend to her neighbors and a generous donor to the American Cancer Society. The problem is that she does exactly these things from the age of 21 to her death at 81. Constance doesn't get better at playing the piano or choose new music. She doesn't grow tired of Land's End fashions. She doesn't get interested in new charities. There is no improvement in any way; there is minimal change. The good she is missing is the good of growth, positive change, progress.

We do seem to value progress itself, and not just the good things that are the outcome of making progress – like greater autonomy, happiness, and accomplishment. Some of the lives we admire most are lives transformed by adversity. Lance Armstrong would impress us if he won the Tour de France over and over again. He impresses us far more because he progressed from cancer survivor to race winner. We're impressed no matter what by a person who is highly autonomous, but we're especially impressed by the great abolitionist Frederick Douglass, who started off as a slave and fought his way to autonomy. Since cancer and slavery are very bad things, and undoubtedly detracted from these two lives, we must accord progress itself a very high value, considering that these lives strike us as being especially good.

We want our lives in some way to go from worse to better. We want that to happen over small stretches and large, in minor ways and in major ways. Moving from worse to better might mean fixing the toaster one morning, or learning salsa dancing in the space of a month, or becoming acquainted with Peru over a summer. Or it could mean becoming a better teacher over a 10-year period, or learning to be more compassionate over a lifetime.

But wouldn't it be better to skip "worse" and go directly to "better" – to have the knowledge, or skills, or activities, or experiences that are "better" from the start? Maybe that would be good for another kind of being. God, in our conception, starts off perfect and stays perfect. Absence of change in a supreme being is no flaw at all. But in us, no progress would be a serious flaw. It's not a fixed toaster, or dancing, or familiarity with Peru that really makes a person's life better. It really is precisely the process of going from broken to fixed, from clumsy to competent, from ignorant to familiar. It's exercising the power to go from worse to better.

In his extraordinary memoir, *Angela's Ashes*, Frank McCourt tells the story of a childhood spent in extreme poverty and heartbreak. He lacks just about every good I've discussed at the beginning of his life, and comes to possess everything as an adult. Is this really a better life than one that starts well and ends well? It certainly is puzzling to say that it is. That would imply that to give our children a shot at the best possible lives, we ought to deliberately put ourselves in dire circumstances. Should we?

It's true that you have a shot at the most extraordinary progress only if you start in the deepest trough. But most people who start in the deepest trough stay there. So, no, we shouldn't seek problems so we can rise to their solutions. If progress is a necessity – and I'm going to say it is, with just a dash of uncertainty – the progress we need is moderate. What we must avoid is complete stagnation. Wherever we start, we should aim higher. It's quite ordinary types of change that we can't do without.

WITH A ROSTER OF good things now in place, let's return for a moment to happiness. Happiness is good wherever it comes from, I've argued, and having some is a necessity. But what if all your happiness comes from valueless sources? Maggie works as a nurse in an intensive care unit. Make her the head nurse so that she has plenty of autonomy. She performs her job impeccably and let's also assume she's a supporter of good causes, perhaps a life-long volunteer at the SPCA. Make it up as you like. She's happy and responsible and she's learned and progressed over time. But here's the hitch. Maggie's happiness comes from Magic Drug. Without it she would find her job grueling, she'd fall into dependent relationships, and she'd hate animals. Magic Drug doesn't just help her derive happiness from her life. It's not like the medication that helped William Styron recover from depression, enabling him to once more derive happiness from his writing and friendships and so on. The source of Maggie's happiness is Magic Drug and nothing else.

Maggie's problem takes plenty of real-world forms. Imagine a person with lots of good in his life, who derives happiness only from gambling. When he's with his lovely wife and children, he's not happy with them, he's happy because he's anticipating the next trip to the casino. (Don't think of this person as an addict, or you'll have trouble believing he has autonomy. No, he's in control of himself. It's just that gambling is his sole source of pleasure.) This strikes me as a blight that stops his life from going entirely well. If he were to stop the gambling and begin to derive satisfaction from spending time with his children (let's say), that would make his life go better.

Happiness is good wherever it comes from, but in addition to wanting happiness, we also want our happiness to come at least substantially from things that have value. The good that Maggie is missing is a funny, subtle sort of thing. There's no one word for it; to have it is to be happy *with* the good things in your life. What we want, beyond happiness and the other things I've discussed, is a link between happiness and the other things. There's no reason for every last drop of our happiness to be derived from valuable things – that would be a rather puritanical expectation – but something's amiss when most of it isn't.

THE LIST SO FAR is missing some wonderful things. What about knowledge? It's crucial for Aristotle, who sees it as one of the valuable fruits of the active life of reason. What about friendship, or love, or affiliation, more generally? It's one of the external goods that Aristotle makes essential to *eudaimonia*. Contemporary list makers sometimes include religion, or something to do with religion. At the other end of the spectrum, some include "play," a heading that encompasses laughter, fun, sport. Some include art, or creativity more generally, or the use of the imagination. In the rest of the chapter, the Aristotelian "missing things" will be the topic; religion is addressed in later chapters; and we'll just have to leave play and imagination for another day.

There's no question that knowledge is vital to living a good life. The indirect contribution it makes is clear, but worth emphasizing. Consider people who come into this country with the assistance of smugglers, who dupe them into indentured servitude. They are given free passage to the United States on the condition of paying later by turning over a part of their paychecks until an exorbitant fee has been paid off. They make this agreement based on many false assumptions: the passage will be safe, the work will not be brutal, the fee will be paid off quickly, more satisfying work will be available later, and there will be a chance to fulfill "the American Dream." Not knowing the truth is life-damaging to say the least. The person who is duped stops being able to control her future. Out of ignorance, she steers herself in entirely the wrong direction: at the very least, toward a desperately miserable existence, and possibly even toward death in a shipping container or in the back of a truck.

In everyday circumstances as well we lose autonomy when we're missing key pieces of information. We need to know the facts about what we're eating or smoking, about the risks we're taking when we choose doctors, medical procedures, travel destinations, forms of recreation, cars, and food. Equally, we need to know fundamental facts about reality. A person who gives shape to her life on the basis of religious beliefs could be involuntarily wasting time, making huge sacrifices, or engaging in senseless ritual if the religious beliefs are false. A person who rejects a supreme being could be getting herself into trouble as a result of *her* beliefs.

Knowing makes an additional indirect contribution because it gives us happiness. Plato, Aristotle, and Mill (among others) stress the pleasures afforded by the intellect. The learned professor loves adding one more gem to his treasure of knowledge. But we all take pleasure in "finding out." Some of our most pleasant moments occur when we are dying of curiosity about something and then suddenly knowledge arrives. Who's going to win the baseball game? When it's over, we finally know, and that feels good. Who is the Unabomber? Who is Johnny's teacher this year? Is the jury going to convict or acquit? Finding out, coming to know – these are great pleasures.

The indirect benefits of knowledge adequately explain why it is to be pursued. But does knowledge itself improve life? There are stories of life going from worse to better that have to do centrally with gaining basic knowledge. By learning to talk and read, Helen Keller comes to have greater and greater awareness of the world around her, and this (along with many other changes), seems to make her life get better.

On the other hand, "fancy" knowledge – what scientists, historians, and other learned people acquire – has an uncertain relationship to life improvement. In Karen Armstrong's memoir, *The Spiral Staircase*, there are many trajectories of improvement. She learns to cope with an illness that once plagued her and caused her misery; she comes to a more confident sense of what she's good at, and therefore who she is; she achieves greater financial independence, and therefore more autonomy. But there's also the trajectory along which she becomes more and more knowledgeable, writing one erudite book about religion after another. Does this improvement, on its own, make her life better? The answer is not so clear. Stories of intellectual achievement elicit admiration, just like stories of emerging artistic talent do. It's enthralling to read about the blossoming of Bob Dylan's musical talent in *Chronicles*, or about Picasso's growth as a painter in his many biographies. The knowledge that Karen Armstrong winds up with, later in life, seems to add to her life in the same way as the artistic genius of Dylan or Picasso. And surely making art and music are not necessities. If knowledge is a necessity, it's basic awareness of the world – what Helen Keller came to have, despite huge obstacles – that's necessary. We needn't all be working our way to intellectual heights, any more than we need to be trying to sing or paint.

If making music, creating art, and acquiring advanced knowledge are not necessary, perhaps they are still fundamentally good, and relevant to the way a life is going. So maybe we have arrived at a point where we must take up the "B" list – the list of things that contribute inter-changeable forms of good. I would also resort to the "B" list when it comes to close relationships. By affirming the role of morality, I have already attached value to the social dimension of human life. A moral person is aware of and concerned about the welfare and rights of other people. But can it be necessary to go further, and actually enter into special relationships with other people? If there are people you love – your children, your spouse, your friends, your parents – it may seem as if having these relationships is essential. But if we stretch be-yond our own personal experience, how can we deny that people who live in solitude can have lives that are basically good – and perhaps great? Relationships add a good to our lives – indeed, a fundamental good. Relationships aren't good because of something else, but for them-selves. But this is a kind of good for which there are substitutes. There are innumerable love stories that are stories of life getting better. But that love dimension can be absent. Karen Armstrong's memoir is a case in point. She does not come to have close love relationships, or children, or even strong friendships. Helen Keller never marries or has children. It seems simply narrow-minded to think these lives are flawed for lack of intimate affiliation.

I'VE ARGUED THAT A life can't go well without happiness, autonomy, self-expression, morality, and progress; and happiness needs to come substantially from good things – we want to be happy *with* the good things in our lives. Basic knowledge or awareness probably belongs on the list as well. Close relationships seem more clearly *not* to belong on the list of necessities; but their value brings to the fore another category of goods – those that are fundamental and relevant, but are merely optional and interchangeable contributors. Perhaps acquiring advanced knowledge, making art, and making music also belong on the "B" list (more on that in Chapter 10).

If the two-list view is correct, then life-getting-better stories are not all the same story. But they are bound to be broadly convergent. I am reminded of the famous first sentence of *Anna Karenina*: "All happy families resemble one another, but each unhappy family is unhappy in its own way." All good lives resemble one another because they have a common core; they are the lives of people who have a modicum of happiness, who run their own lives to some considerable degree, who are basically responsible, and so on. But lives that are not good are not good in different ways. They can be not good because of misery, or because of an extreme dearth of autonomy, or because of moral reprehensibility. Thus, stories that trace the path from not good to good focus on different paths. The story of recovery from a depression is not the same as the story of escape from slavery, which is not the story of coming to take responsibility for one's actions.

Then again, it's just at the core that good lives converge. There are innumerable ways of being happy, running your life, and taking responsibility. Furthermore, there's the added variety of the "B" list. We'll see in Chapter 10 what we might put on that list, but if things like intellectual and artistic achievement fit in there, all the more reason to expect good lives to be varied. It's not common for all the "B" list goods to be concentrated in one life. In fact, it might not even be possible, because some of the optional goods may in fact be incompatible with others. As I'll argue in Chapter 10, balance seems to add something to life, but so do focus and intensity, and these are virtues that tend to be the virtues of different lives.

The two lists have some practical value. If they're anything like correct, they show that happiness is not everything; that autonomy is not everything. With these lists providing guidance, we would know that living ethically is not something we do entirely for the benefit of others, but for ourselves as well. We would know that we mustn't stagnate, or spend all our time amusing ourselves in pointless ways, or live our lives in sheer imitation of the way other people live their lives. We would know all sorts of things. But not everything. Unfortunately, life frequently puts us in situations that force us to make hard choices. If personal happiness comes at the price of morality in some specific situation, which comes first? If more autonomy means less growth and progress, which matters more? These are the kinds of questions that will come next.

But before turning to questions of choice, we'll take up something even more fundamental. The "A" list is curious. Are the things on the list really necessities for every human being, or even for all living creatures? If they're necessities even just for one person, there's a second question. What makes any good on the list indispensable; why can't lots of one make up for shortages of others? These two questions will turn out to be related, as we'll see in Chapter 6.

Chapter 6

—— Puzzles of Diversity ——

Is there one list of necessities that defines what it is to live well no matter who you are, where you live, whether you have all the normal human abilities or whether you're severely disabled? Does the very same standard apply even when the lives in question are not human, but animal lives? That would be extraordinary, but it's not impossible. To find our way to a reasonable answer, we need to look more closely at what it means for any asset to be *necessary*.

How do things like happiness, autonomy, morality, and the rest endow a life with goodness? The answer seems simple. The goodness of the critical ingredients "infects" the life as a whole. The more good stuff you add to a life, the more it becomes overall good. At least that's a beginning. Yet there's one way in which this explanation is incomplete. If it's just a matter of good ingredients infecting the whole, then why is it that a ton of one ingredient doesn't have the power to substitute for shortages of others? Why isn't an evil person able to make up for a shortage of morality by being extremely happy? Why can't we do without autonomy, if we've got a lot of progress and growth?

Each thing on the list from the last chapter seems to be not merely one source of good, capable of increasing a whole life's goodness, but a necessity. What we need to get a grip on is what this necessity is all about. Once we have a grip on necessity, we'll be able to see whether it's really true that the same things are necessities in every conceivable life.

The question is particularly urgent in the case of disabilities. A person with disabilities could be limited in her ability to fill her life with some of the good things on Chapter 5's list, because of the way she is (whether innately or as a result of some injury or illness). It's tempting to think some of these things are unnecessary for her. Are there different lists of necessities for different individuals, based on differing abilities and disabilities? What we say here will be felt acutely by readers who have disabilities, or care for people who do, or worry that someday they will. A position can inspire rage, or the opposite. That might be a reason to employ that most popular of academic phrases, "beyond the scope of this book," but the fact is that it isn't. One list for all or many different lists depending on abilities? That's a question at the very core of my subject.

PHILOSOPHER PETER SINGER HAS paid a high price for saying the "wrong" thing. The author of many important and influential books in ethics, covering topics like animal rights, abortion, euthanasia, and our responsibilities to people in developing countries, it wasn't surprising when Singer was offered a job at Princeton's Center for Human Values in 1999. But the offer stirred up relentless protest from disability rights advocates. Here was a man well known among philosophers for urging compassion for animals and famine victims, for recognizing the equality of all creatures, rich and poor, black and white, human and non-human; yet people with disabilities were demonstrating wherever he went. At the end of the second edition of his most comprehensive book, *Practical Ethics*, Singer describes especially rough treatment in Germany, where his lectures started being flooded by protesters, or outright banned, as far back as 1990. Singer describes the pain of being treated as a kind of neo-Nazi, when three of his own grandparents were killed in concentration camps by real Nazis. At one lecture he was drowned out by chanting protesters, one of whom approached the podium and actually knocked off his glasses.

What did Singer say about disabilities to elicit such hostility? One thing he said is that people with very severe disabilities are likely to live lives that are not as good. The starting point for Singer's assessment is a notion of what makes lives go well or badly that's similar to the desire-fulfillment theory discussed in Chapter 4. If you are blind, or confined to a wheelchair, or you suffer from an intellectual disability, there are very likely things you want but can't obtain. You might have frustrated desires to walk, read more quickly, succeed in a profession, find a romantic partner, become happier. These frustrations, on the desire-fulfillment theory, are significant. They make your life worse than the lives of people with fewer frustrations.

Singer's views would have offended some readers, but probably would not have attracted wide attention if it weren't for the way that they connect to questions about euthanasia. Singer thinks the reduced potential to live a good life in a disabled infant can sometimes (with lots of qualifications) give parents a legitimate reason to want the child's life to be terminated; and he thinks that the law should not stand in their way. In short, in certain cases, he would permit the killing of severely disabled infants, if it were all up to him. It's not nice to be told that your disability is such a blight that your mother would have been blameless had she chosen to kill you when you were an infant.

Saying this seems out of step with Singer's characteristic compassion, but in fact at the root of his position is sympathy for the players in a not uncommon medical drama. A couple is expecting a child. No pre-natal testing is done because the mother is too young to be at significant risk of having a baby with genetic problems. Perhaps her obstetrician has told her that amniocentesis poses a slight risk of causing a miscarriage. On ultrasound, things look fine. But the baby is born with a disability and the disability is so serious that there's no possibility of finding adoptive parents. The burden of raising this child will prevent the couple from having another, or will at least draw time and resources from any second child. The parents want to give the child a lethal injection. It sounds horrible, but Singer sympathizes. The parents' preference is not beyond the pale. If the baby had a physical problem that required immediate attention, the physician might accede to the parents' wishes (wink, wink) and allow the baby to die – and even die painfully. If it's better for the baby to die, isn't it better to bring about the death in the kindest, quickest manner?

At the very least, I think we ought to share Singer's sympathy with these parents. But there's more to his position than sympathy; there are complicated arguments, some of which really are "beyond the scope of this book." The part of Singer's view that is relevant here is just one premise, the one that says being severely disabled tends to mean living a life that's not as good. Had he said no more than that, he might not have found himself in the limelight, but he would have given plenty of offense.

One person Singer has offended is Harriet McBryde Johnson, who first encountered Singer in 2001, when he spoke at Charleston College in

South Carolina. Johnson was one of the protesters in wheelchairs, but not one of the people trying to silence Singer. In fact, she went to his lecture and asked penetrating questions. After further e-mail contact, Singer invited her to Princeton, where they talked at length. Johnson maintains a disability law practice and also writes for a living. After years of muscle wasting, she is confined to a wheelchair and relies on attendants to help her with the tasks of daily living. Johnson is unwilling to agree that disabilities make life worse; not even severe disabilities.

But of course they do, argues Singer. There's just no denying it. If a child born with a disability had just the same prospects as any other child, it would be no big deal for a woman to drink during pregnancy, despite the link between alcohol and fetal alcohol syndrome (which includes mental retardation). The sleeping pill thalidomide would still be in use, even though it's a known teratogen. We all know that it's wrong to knowingly cause an infant to be born with disabilities. And that means that Singer is right that life is usually worse for the disabled.

Johnson's response to Singer is well worth reading – she wrote about her conversations with him in the *New York Times Magazine* and in a subsequent book, *Too Late to Die Young*. As Singer notes in *Practical Ethics*, many of his critics don't bother to read what he's written. Johnson is well versed in Singer's writings. She also comes to her reading of Singer from a position that's not worlds apart. An atheist like Singer is, she doesn't respond to his straightforward points with foggy allusions to the sanctity of life. She meets him head on.

Yes, if a child is coming into the world, a mother shouldn't knowingly diminish his abilities, but the reason is not what Singer says it is. She shouldn't stunt him (says Johnson) because the world reacts to the disabled with fear, discomfort, prejudice, and insufficient accommodation. The disabled person is not constitutionally but socially disadvantaged. Being disabled is a bit like being short (my example). If drinking Coke during pregnancy would make your child short, you'd probably not drink Coke, because our society treats short people less kindly. But being short doesn't inherently reduce a person's prospects for a good life. Nor does being disabled.

Some disabled people see things differently. Before his death, actor Christopher Reeve ardently wished to regain the abilities he had lost in a devastating horse-riding accident. He wanted to walk not just so people would stop staring at him, or because there are too few wheelchair ramps. He thought his life would be better if he could walk again. His very public support for research to heal spinal cord injuries made Reeve no hero in Johnson's eyes. In effect, he betrayed people like her, who demand that we see living with a disability as living a perfectly good life.

If there's one list of necessities for all people, the result is a verdict on the lives of the severely (and irreversibly) disabled that's like Singer's – though starting from different premises. We will have to say their lives cannot go as well, because they have much less of, or sometimes none of, some of the good things on the list. Some disabilities reduce happiness or impair important aspects of autonomy or preclude meaningful types of growth and progress or eliminate the potential for morality – or all of the above (and more). On the other hand, if there are different lists for different people, we are moving in the direction of Johnson. If their lives are judged by separate standards, differently abled people can achieve equal success. To decide which way to go, we will withdraw from the full-blooded drama of Singer vs. Johnson, and back up to the more basic question about necessity. Why is any asset ever necessary in a person's life, instead of merely being an optional contributor of one type of value?

We might say each good on the "A" list is a necessity because each is so fundamental – so absolutely essential to living a good life. On some deep conceptual level, there's just no such thing as a good life without each one of them. Of course, that would lead to the idea that the necessary ingredients for one life are the same as for any other, and to the less optimistic view of living with a disability.

This view has quite a bit of plausibility when it comes to *one* of the goods on the list. A life devoid of happiness is either unconscious or constantly miserable, or continually neutral, and in no case good. If that endearing Vulcan, Mr. Spock, really never felt any emotion (except in one episode of *Star Trek*), not even the low hum of mild happiness, what could his life have been like? Not so good, I think. We're not in a rush to judge Spock's life harshly, but that's because by all *appearances* he feels at least much of what human beings do. (That's part of the fun of the theme of Spock's unemotionality.) A person who genuinely felt nothing, or nothing positive, really would have a very limited existence.

The most radical disability activists are not prepared to find fault with any human existence. Even a person presumably without any conscious experience, due to a severe neurological impairment, must not be thought to live a life any worse than anyone else's. I'm skeptical that it's possible to reason one's way to such a conclusion. Those who embrace it refuse to make distinctions because they think all lives are equally sacred, or because they think it's simply too dangerous to make any distinctions. Singer's German critics are understandably reluctant to downgrade any person's potential, considering their collective memory of horrifying Nazi eugenics programs, only 60 years ago.

But conscious experience does seem like an absolute necessity; and it also seems necessary for experience to have, to some degree, a positive quality. A life without consciousness seems not worth living, and one that's devoid of all enjoyment seems at least flawed.

Could you attach the same sort of *absolute* necessity to every good thing on the "A" list from Chapter 5? It's not hard to imagine a life that goes well without morality. Very young children live part of their lives well without any sense of right and wrong. The story of Adam and Eve depicts a time before there is "knowledge of good and evil" and yet life is glorious. If we expect morality in ordinary lives, that's not because no conceivable life *could* be good without it. The same goes for autonomy and self-expression, and many of the other ingredients I've discussed.

So what makes these things necessary? In some places, both Aristotle and John Stuart Mill argue that we should aim for those good things that make us human (both also suggest in places that we should aim for what's best – human or not – and we've seen that Mill is a sometimes advocate of the Simple Happiness Theory.) We live better lives the more we perfect ourselves as human beings – i.e. the more that we attain the defining assets. The idea is that a good life for X is a life in which X does a particularly good job of being what X is: in the case of a human being, being an especially fine specimen of a human being.

My "A" list could be given this sort of interpretation. Morality, autonomy, and so on, are the *kinds* of things that might be regarded as definitive of our humanity. If we looked at things this way, we'd have to say that a life is flawed when it's missing any one of these assets because it's less than a fully human life. The implications for the way we think about living with disabilities are pretty easy to see.

Certainly, some disabilities don't create a barrier to achieving the things on the "A" list. Harriet McBryde Johnson may very well live a life amply endowed with them all – even autonomy, if the most meaningful forms of autonomy involve planning your own life, choosing your own path, being in charge of yourself. But imagine a young adult with Down's syndrome whom I'll call "Carlos." People with Down's syndrome have a very wide spectrum of capacities, but I'm going to assume his case is severe. He is so cognitively impaired that he has little ability to live autonomously; many of his choices are made for him. He really doesn't understand morality at all. When he's not closely supervised, he steals small things, or perhaps he tells occasional lies. And he does these things without remorse. Nevertheless, let's assume he's sociable, and cheerful, and he can learn and grow – just not in exactly the way that most people can. Since he'll never attain many of the things on my list, and he won't be able to move in the direction of perfecting himself as a human being, we've got to be pessimistic about his prospects for a good life.

This is discomforting, but that's not the reason we should reject the goal of being fully human. We should reject it because it really doesn't hold water. The things that make us human are not just esteemed things like morality and autonomy. Perhaps "a touch of evil" is more human than scrupulous morality. Jonathan Glover named his history of the moral atrocities of the twentieth century *"Humanity,"* not *"Inhumanity,"* and sadly enough, there's something right about his title. Everywhere and at all times, human beings have been complicit in so many horrors that we can't possibly exclude immorality from the spectrum of truly human possibilities. Should we aspire to some balance of good and evil, just because that will make us consummately human?

Another problem is that "human" covers biological features we have little reason to aim for. In the Isaac Asimov story *Bicentennial Man* (made into a movie with Robin Williams in the lead role), a robot gradually becomes more and more human-like. "Andrew" possesses conscious thought and emotion; he's capable of love and exquisite sensitivity. Eventually he devotes himself to erasing the last vestiges of his electronic origins. He has his body modified so that he'll age. But that's not enough for the world president, who refuses to recognize him as a human being. Finally, Andrew has his body reconfigured so that he'll "achieve" human mortality. "How can it be worth it, Andrew? You're a fool," says a fellow robot. "If it brings me humanity, that will be worth it," says Andrew. Only when he is dead does the world president declare him human. The reader has to wonder whether it was really worth it. Wasn't his life just as good (in fact, better) before he became fully human – and dead?

The contrast between human and non-human does not enter into our decision making often. Perhaps you love to run, and you devote a lot of your energy to being the best runner you can be. Would it give you pause if someone pointed out to you that running is not particularly human? That your astonishing running is making you resemble a gazelle or a cheetah? That there are other pastimes that are more distinctively human?

In spite of the common use of the word "human" as an honorific, as a synonym for all that is worth aspiring to, it's not at all obvious that being human is an ambition we do have or should have. We are simply human, whatever our abilities or disabilities, however much we use them or don't use them. To be especially human is an odd and questionable goal.

LET'S MAKE THE PUZZLE about necessities as vivid as possible. Imagine a ballerina who works hard to please a domineering company director; make the story one in which he controls every aspect of her life, telling her what to eat, how to dress, who to spend her time with. Under his tutelage, she makes rapid progress as a dancer. Let's make autonomy the only thing she lacks; she's actually quite happy as a puppet, and she manages to hold on to a strong sense of who she is, despite being pushed around all the time. The pile of good in her life reaches impressive heights, but it's missing breadth. She doesn't have the kind of good that's involved in being able to make choices about what to do, where to go, who to consort with, what to say. Why insist on that particular kind of good, if her life is so well endowed with the other kinds of good? Why is autonomy a necessity?

The answer I'm going to propose is very simple. The ballerina has a capacity for autonomy and it's going completely to waste; autonomy is too good a thing, and too fundamental, to be squandered. She shouldn't waste her own capacity for autonomy, and the world around her shouldn't force her to waste it. When that capacity does go to waste, the result is an injury to the overall goodness of the dancer's life. We cannot say her life quite rises to the level of being basically good.

There is a kernel of truth in the self-help books' advice to fulfill our potential, and to the Marines' motto, "Be all that you can be." If something profoundly good is within your grasp, then reach for it! The imperative is to make an effort in the direction of the good things that are available to *you* as you actually are. So the facts about your abilities and disabilities do make a difference.

This does need a bit of clarifying. I wouldn't go as far as to say that all potentials must be exploited. The imperative is – only – not to allow our potentials for great good to go completely to waste. It couldn't be that we ought to exercise all of our abilities, because there are just too many of them. We couldn't even be obligated to try, for then we would be dashing from violin lessons to skating lessons to cooking class, doing a tiny bit of a thousand things. It also doesn't seem that we must exploit the potentials that make us unique. If I'm one of the few who can draw, then I shouldn't waste the talent to draw, we may think. But that has mostly to do with obligations to others. If "the team" needs someone to draw, and I'm the only member who can do it, then I might owe it to the team to draw. As far as my own good goes, I have no obligation to use an ability that happens to be rare. The notion that we ought to exhaust our potential also seems to misinterpret the imperative to use our potential. Not using a potential at all is a very different thing from failing to use every last drop of it.

It's the breadth and value of an ability that makes it important to make at least some use of it. I am reminded of the motto of the United Negro College Fund: "A mind is a terrible thing to waste." The motto is not: "The ability to learn calculus is a terrible thing to waste." We should not equate the waste of restricted, small-scale abilities with the waste of all of one's ability to be happy, or self-expressive, or moral, or to learn. To waste the ability to make fondue is one thing; to waste the ability to run your own life is another. But ultimately, the difference is just one of degree. More value means more of a problem with squandering. The goods I put on the "A" list in the last chapter seem to have this kind of special value. We ought to pursue happiness, autonomy, self-expression, and the rest, because they are very broad categories of good – they cover a lot – and they are especially good. The goods I put on the "B" list seem less broad and less valuable. It's not as much of a waste if a child never receives any art materials or art education, and can't make art. It's a huge waste if a child is born into slavery, and never has a chance to exercise any control over his life.

Perhaps you can agree that we ought not to entirely waste an extremely precious, broad class of abilities. I'm even hoping that you agree that this reasoning backs my list of necessary life ingredients. But now, let us consider a reservation, before returning to the lives of people with disabilities. Aren't there some very broad and super-valuable things that have been left off the "A" list? Take, for example, the ability to reproduce. The power to make human beings is pretty marvelous. And so don't we have to exploit it, if we have to exploit all profoundly good capacities? And doesn't that mean you can't live a good life if you can have children but decide not to? And isn't that absurd?

The crucial question is whether the ability to reproduce really is so very good that we must speak of squandered potential when it isn't used. That way of looking at things is not completely off track. When a child dies, I think the many potentials that did not get fulfilled are part of the tragedy, and one focal point is the unfulfilled potential to have children. A person who wants to bear children, and cannot, may feel frustration that centers, not irrationally, on a sense of unused potential. Not using a potential for good, however large or small, is always a pity, to some degree. But it cannot be said that having children is always a much better thing than not having children. Each has its advantages. A new child is something wonderful, of course. But being childless, in our overpopulated world, can actually make myriad tiny differences for the better. Because that decision is made, in the future there is a bit less drain on natural resources, a bit less overcrowding in schools. Each of the benefits is minor, but they add up. A slight improvement to the lives of a very large number of people over many years might be as good as the creation of one new life. I don't think a person has to create new lives rather than bettering other lives. And when we don't fill our time with the job of parenting, a frequent result is more room for other good things – whether it's enjoying a close marriage, producing more and better art, caring for animals, or being especially self-expressive.

Are the items on my "A" list *all* the things that are so good and fundamental and broad that they shouldn't be wasted? I'm open to persuasion about other goods that should be on the list, but inevitably there's some vagueness that has to be tolerated. There's no sharp line between the good things that are so broad and so extremely good that they should not be wasted, and the things that are merely good. There are surely things that fall in between, not obviously qualifying for the "A" list, but appearing to be more critical than other things on the "B" list. That's something we have to live with. These are not mathematical questions, and we should not expect mathematically precise answers.

So WHAT ABOUT CARLOS? To think about his life, we must understand what potentials he wastes or exploits, and that means we must know what potentials he really starts out with. Carlos's actual abilities are the ones that count. I described him as having little capacity for autonomy or morality. That means that, while the lack of autonomy in the life of the ballerina left her life flawed, the very same lack of autonomy in the life of Carlos is another matter. The ballerina was forced to waste her potential for autonomy. In Carlos's life, there is no wasted potential. Where we do fault a person who could have exercised moral responsibility, but didn't use that potential, we will not fault Carlos for his moral lapses. These mistakes leave no gap, create no flaw.

Applying different standards to different people, our perspective will be relativistic, in one sense of the word. We will have a notion of the good life *for Carlos*. But we will not be reverting to the sort of relativism discussed in Chapter 2. We will not be giving up on making independent judgments; we will not be automatically deferring to the opinions of the person whose life we are examining; we will not be deferring to cultural standards. The idea is to use the right standard for each person, the standard that's appropriately tailored to that person's abilities. For most human beings, the relevant standard is the same. For human beings who are differently abled, the standard is different.

Martha Nussbaum's view on these issues in *Frontiers of Justice* contrasts with mine. She thinks that a separate sense of the important capabilities, tailored to disabilities, will inevitably foster unfairly low expectations and a derogatory sense that the disabled aren't quite human. As I've already argued, I don't set much store by the aspiration to be human. Genetically, that's what we all simply are, whether we're disabled or not. It's true that we shouldn't sell anyone short, and that bias against the disabled puts us in danger of doing so. What seems like a far greater danger is forcing Carlos to take up activities that are meaningless to him, if a single set of necessities is held up as a universal standard; and then finding Carlos pitiful when he falls short. Where Nussbaum sees dignity in sheer humanness, I see dignity in doing all that you can do, whatever else others might be capable of doing.

At this point it's starting to look as if the prospects for people with disabilities are just like anyone else's because everyone should be regarded against a background of their own individual potentials. Singer's pessimistic view of living with a severe disability is turning out to be wrong, and Johnson's optimistic view is turning out to be right. But now the plot really must thicken.

If there's no morality in Carlos's life, that doesn't mean he's missing anything that's necessary *for him*. The pile of good in his life has the proper breadth. But it does mean there are fewer types of good that can add bulk to the pile of good in his life. If there's less autonomy and less progress, again, that means those types of good can't add to the bulk. Breadth matters, but bulk matters too. We want lots of good in our lives, not simply all the necessary kinds.

Must the sheer amount of good in Carlos's life be low, as a result of his disabilities? Well, no. If you take the higher intellectual capacities away from a life, there might be more room for unfettered happiness. The sheer quantity of good in Carlos's life could actually be unusually great. But is there any guarantee? Again, no. In her book *Too Late to Die Young*, Johnson refuses to force the story of her life into one of the molds that people would like it to fill. One of the molds insists everything is for the best; that a big problem here is always made up for by a huge asset there. If you've got a lot less of one good thing, you must have a lot more of another good thing. You might, but it's just not true that you must. It does seem plausible that removing capacities from a life some-times reduces the total good. But what does that mean: 48 percent of the time? 63 percent of the time?

A young man I know has a moderate intellectual impairment. At the age when most of his peers are heading for college, "Stephen" has a job bagging groceries at a natural foods store. His "normal" brother has just married and is about to receive an advanced degree in mathematics. I've never met the brother, but would it make sense for me to suppose his life is going better? Prejudice and disrespect are forces that incline us to say, "Yes." But of course they should be resisted. From what I can tell, Stephen is thriving in the areas that are meaningful for him. The sheer quantity of good in his life could conceivably be especially great. His disability holds him back in some areas, but he's warm, sociable, and by all appearances very happy. My way of looking at things stops us – and I think rightly – from jumping to the conclusion that this is an unfortunate life.

Still, the total good in a life is reduced by disabilities often enough to explain why they are to be avoided. As Singer sensibly points out, preg-nant women really should do everything they can to avoid reducing their babies' capacities. It's reasonable for obstetricians to advise them not to drink, since alcohol can cause intellectual impairment, among other problems. The reason is not just that disabilities are met with prejudice but that on the whole it's better not to have them. At the same time, we need to recognize that each individual case is distinctive, and that good lives don't fit into just one mold.

IF THE NECESSITIES FOR any individual's life vary depending upon abilities and disabilities, we are able to look at living with disabilities in a way that's intermediate between Singer and Johnson. This seems to be just where we want our perspective to fall. But let's not be too comfortable too soon. There are some worries that ought to be confronted.

It could be that you've had a nagging doubt for a while. Say a person has no capacity for moral choice: he's a demented, remorseless, socio-pathic serial killer (fill in more details as you please). Should we really say his life is just fine, so long as he has heaps of other sorts of good in his life? That sounds like a verdict we would want to avoid!

You could avoid this verdict by saying morality is an absolute neces-sity, but I already argued against that. You could avoid it by saying there's one human essence we all should try to perfect, and it includes morality. But I've argued against that. Have I painted myself into a corner? That's a worrisome possibility!

In fact, I think we are not really stuck with a positive evaluation of any real sociopaths – but at most the ones that live inside of very unrealistic hypotheticals. We imagined a sociopath whose life is full of immorality, but also full of good things. I think we must reconsider whether that's a realistic possibility. It would be if the sociopath were a wolf. A wolf can violently attack innocent humans, cheat on his wife, neglect his children, and be disloyal to friends and yet have all the good that can be expected in his life. The sociopath is not a wolf. If he commits all the same crimes, the community around him will not like it one bit. He will land in prison, lose autonomy, productivity, and happiness. In all the other-than-moral respects, his life will start to go badly.

No doubt, the possibility of a very secretive sociopath comes to mind – a person who is a serial killer by night, and an upstanding citizen by day. In this case, do we have to bite the bullet and say that his life really is going well for him? Clearly, the secretive sociopath is a menace to everyone else and we have every reason to hunt him down and lock him up. But must we say the hypothetical happy, well-adjusted, super-stealthy sociopath leads a life that, for him, is a good life?

It's safe to say that we don't have to swallow such claims about any *actual* secretive sociopaths. Even if a real-world sociopath's crimes never come to light, it's most likely they would have a distorting effect on his whole life. He will try to control himself, for fear of being caught; his inability to control himself will make him not so autonomous. The double life he lives compromises his happiness, and surely (I am speculating), his wicked deeds don't actually give him unalloyed enjoyment. The energy he puts into trying to control and hide the secret side of himself is siphoned from everything else he attempts to do. As a result of this, his life is not flawed because of his immorality (he has no capacity to be otherwise), but his life is bound to be flawed because he wastes the many capacities that he does have; and because the sum of good in his life from all sources winds up being very small.

It might still seem odd not to see this man's immorality as a life defect, but that's the price of seeing Carlos the way we did. We assumed he had no capacity for morality either. The right thing to say – or so it seems – is that Carlos's small-scale crimes don't create even small flaws in his life; the critical fact is that he has no capacity for morality. But then, to be consistent, we can't see the sociopath's big crimes as creating big flaws in this life. He has no capacity for morality either. The point I've made is that the sociopath's crimes are bound to thoroughly damage his life. Indirectly, they do rob him of the chance to live a good life. That's all that we can say, but maybe it's enough.

IF A GOOD LIFE is different things, depending on individual abilities, then that means a good life will certainly be different things in different species. Let's depart from the subject of human abilities and disabilities and turn to animal lives, briefly.

Don't scoff at the idea that animals can live good lives and bad lives. Of course you won't catch a dog sitting in a café reading this book. He's not going to be forced to take stock of his life because he's lost his job or because his puppies are leaving home. You're the one who has decisions to make that affect animals. You have to decide whether it's OK to keep your dog in a crate while you're at work. You have to give thought to the lives of cats when you decide whether to keep your cats inside or let them out, whether to declaw them or not, whether to have them

THE WEIGHT OF THINGS

neutered. You have to think about animal lives when you decide whether to keep fish in a tank or gerbils in a cage. Anyone involved in zoo keeping or wildlife management or animal agriculture must have some notion of what a reasonably good life encompasses, for the species in question. Medical researchers have to give thought to these issues when they decide which species to experiment on, or whether to experiment on animals at all; and when they decide what are reasonable standards to maintain in the laboratory.

When we look at animal lives, I don't think we've moved into entirely new territory. Once more, happiness is a necessity for any species. A species that truly feels nothing has no life to speak of, and we cannot distinguish good lives from bad lives. If cockroaches feel nothing, go ahead and sprinkle boric acid on your baseboards. It matters little that your cockroaches will be badly inconvenienced, not to mention being poisoned to death. Environments that promote happiness make animal lives go better. Birds shouldn't be in cages that stop them from flying because there's pleasure in flying (I'm 99 percent sure). When we're not blinded by the desire for cheap, tasty meat, it's obvious that farm animals live better lives when they get a chance to enjoy moving their limbs out-of-doors.

In most species, there is considerable capacity for autonomy, and an animal cannot live a good life without fulfilling it at least to some degree. A pig cannot live a good life stuck in a stall where it can't move; a chicken can't live a good life packed 20 to a cage; your dog can't live a good life in a crate; your cat can't live as good a life in the house – although you've got to juggle quantity of life vs. quality of life before you decide whether to let him out. Autonomy counts in the lives of animals.

I might even sign on for a third ingredient as being important in some animal lives. I said in Chapter 5 that we want to be happy with the good things in our lives. Happiness is always good, but it's a further good when it comes from good sources, not from a pill or some other vacuous source. Likewise, it seems better when an animal is happy because of his life activities, and not because he's receiving happiness injections. I know you're thinking this has no real-world application. But it does. It seems like a crated dog is not entirely helped toward a better life if he's given Prozac by his psychiatrist (yes, this is an option). You can't entirely solve the problem of raising pigs with awful lives by altering them so that they don't feel miserable packed into narrow stalls – though agricultural corporations are trying to genetically engineer pigs like that. Yes, it's good to be happy, but it seems better to be happy with frolicking in the sun and digging for truffles than to be happy with . . . what? . . . spending the whole day in the dark, nibbling on the tail of the pig in front of you.

Learning and progress . . . do they occur in the lives of animals? The growth from immaturity to maturity seems as positive for animals as it is for us. In some species, the young learn to master essential behaviors by observing their parents. Graduating to independence seems like a plus for a chimpanzee, as it is for a teenager. On the other hand, it's not so obvious that *externally* imposed progress makes any difference to animals themselves. People who devote years and years of effort to teaching bonobos a little sign language don't seem to do much of a favor to the animal. I have a hunch the bonobo would just as soon be living in the wild, enjoying the wildly promiscuous life that comes naturally to him. Maybe lions find it more interesting being trained to do circus tricks, instead of languishing in a cage all day, but the progress the lion makes seems to give him no advantage over a wild animal. The exception might be domesticated animals that have evolved to have a close relationship with humans. Maybe becoming a skilled guide dog or a winning thoroughbred is good for dog and horse.

Forming and expressing a self? Morality? Neither seems to have much application to the lives of animals, although there may be a kind of proto-morality in social animals. But then, some of the goods that did not seem like necessities for us might be necessities for animals. The capacity to reproduce does not seem to be something we have to exercise, and part of the reason is that not exercising it makes room for the fulfillment of other potentials. Last time I looked, sterilized and puppyless dogs weren't making use of the extra time to write novels. Maybe we do limit the lives of individual animals when we stop them from reproducing. But surely we do so with justification – we're trying to reduce the population of neglected animals who wind up being euthanized at animal shelters.

The necessities, for a good animal life, depend on the species, and they are different from the necessities in a good human life. We cannot, with any logic, complain that an animal lives a life that is not self-expressive, or not responsible. An animal doesn't need to be these things. On the other hand, because there is less potential for good things in the life of an animal, there are also fewer ways to add to the heap of good in an animal's life. All the good there will be is happiness-good, autonomy-good, and so on. And that heap could wind up having smaller bulk than a human being's, as a result.

But need it have smaller bulk? In the same way happiness in the life of the cognitively impaired can be greater because of the impairment, an animal's happiness could be greater because of his nature. I wouldn't mind spending a day or two living with the heightened sense of smell of a wolf, or being able to fly like a bird, or having the irrepressible, guilt-free sex drive of a bonobo. Wouldn't it be delightful to be innately endowed with the ability to fend for yourself in the wild, instead of doing a job all day, getting slips of paper in return, exchanging the slips for edibles, and then assembling them into meals? It could be delightful grazing in a pasture or chasing and killing dinner in some remote, unspoiled forest. Or swimming around in the depths of the sea, sucking up krill, or maybe dining (guilt-free, of course) on the occasional surfer.

Recognizing good in the lives of animals has a great deal of practical importance. It might make us think twice about the chimpanzees in primate research centers, who are infected with the HIV virus (or more precisely, the Simian analogue) and then observed, over many years, in the confines of their cages. These animals are forced to live very bad lives, when they could have lived good lives – good for many of the same reasons our lives can be good. Appreciating their lives isn't all there is to solving the moral quandary about experimenting on them, but it's relevant.

And then, on the other hand, the perspective on animal lives I'm offering might put you more at ease about experimenting on mice and rats. For we certainly would be off base if we found their lives lacking because they weren't capable of morality and self-expression. But we could be right if we said the heap of good in their lives is fairly small in bulk. I can imagine huge amounts of happiness in the life of a lion. The much smaller-brained mouse seems to have a less interesting life. But I could be wrong. Darting about in small spaces seems like no fun to me, but maybe it's marvelous for a mouse.

So much for the question of necessity – why you can't make up for a dearth of one thing by having heaps and heaps of another. I've argued that if you tried, you'd wind up wasting a potential for fundamental good. The flip side of the coin is that the necessities are not the same for every life. They depend on abilities. That is particularly relevant if we are thinking about the lives of people with disabilities; it's also central to thinking about the lives of animals.

But what about when it comes to different individuals? What there is to make use of or waste varies between species, and between groups within a species. Isn't there also significant variation from one individual to another?

Surely there is, and it makes some difference. I don't think it's a great shame if making art is a (largely) wasted ability in me, because my ability to make art is nothing extraordinary. It certainly seems as if it would have been much more of a shame if Picasso's art-making ability had been wasted. If wasting is bad in the case of profound goods like autonomy, it's got to be at least somewhat bad in the case of anything that's good, and quite bad when a capacity is very good. Still, I think the goods I've focused on have a special status. As great as artistic talent is, it's not on a par with the fundamental power to run your own life. The kind of goods that are so good that we think they absolutely mustn't be wasted are things that are (fortunately) quite evenly distributed among normal human beings. As for the other good things – art, music, and the like – more needs to be said about them, but they'll remain in the background until Chapter 10.

We'll turn now to the nature of choice. How we choose among fundamentally different things is a pertinent question whenever necessities are multiple. The backdrop for the discussion could be any list of necessities. It could be the list for Carlos, or the list for Picasso. But I'll return to the original list from Chapter 5 – the main things that constitute necessities for most of us. If all those things are necessary, and we are forced to pursue one at the expense of another, how are we to choose?

Chapter 7

Hard Choices

A very lucky person could live a good life without ever giving any direct attention to the ultimate things that make lives go well or unwell. Laws, institutions, customs, and plain good fortune could keep her continually pointed in the right direction, so that she effortlessly came by ample happiness, autonomy, self-expression, and the rest. Even in less fortuitous circumstances, we don't wrestle with choices between ultimate things very often. If we are torn between different ways of going forward, we're more likely to be struggling between law school and art school, or between family and work, than to be thinking in terms of competing ultimate goods, like autonomy and self-expression. It's much the same with dietary dilemmas: you're more likely to feel torn between apple pie and chocolate cake than to worry over vitamin C and calcium. It takes things going wrong, to some degree, to be snared in a life dilemma, and it takes a pretty intractable dilemma for a person to begin dissecting what his options really offer him, in ultimate terms. But it happens. And it's worth considering what goes into the most fundamental choices.

Penelope is a mother of three children. Her children are getting older and more independent, and she comes to feel that she has too much time on her hands. Looking for a chance to "grow," she decides to go back to college, pursuing the degree she abandoned years earlier. Her classes open up new worlds and expose her to interesting people. But soon she discovers that she's inundated by class assignments. She can't spend the time with her children that she wants to. A fastidious housekeeper, the beds aren't even being made. At first the problem is about homework and soccer games and dirty dishes and other minutiae, but as she wrestles with it, the colors of the problem change. What it's really about is her autonomy, which seems threatened by the return to school – she feels like she's losing control – and personal growth, which is enhanced. The dilemma could be about other things as well – what should she do to cultivate and express her own identity? What will make her happiest? If her problem seems difficult enough to her, she may come to think about it in all of these terms.

A special kind of dilemma pits what is morally better against what is morally worse. You feel a moral obligation to spend more time with your children, but it's also good, in other ways, to train for triathlons. It would make you happy to spend loads of money on a big TV, but the same money would save many lives in a developing country. Here things are especially tricky. Morality compels in a different way than the other good things. We ought to pursue our own happiness, and autonomy and so on, for many reasons. These things are good. They shouldn't go to waste. The path to having a better life is through pursuing them. You can say the same things about morality, but there is an extra reason to make the morally best choice. It's simply the right thing to do. And so when we are torn between morality and anything else, morality might always take priority. We'll take up that possibility in the next chapter.

For now, we'll take morality off the list, and look at situations that pit the other goods against each other. Torn between different fundamentally good things, how are we to choose? Can choices be made with any objectivity, or are they entirely subjective? Are decisions about our own lives amenable to reason, or are they largely emotional? We will begin with dilemmas of contemporary life and then move back a century and a half, to the painfully difficult choices of American slaves, men and women who could only achieve autonomy at the cost of enormous suffering.

JOHN FINNIS IS A contemporary philosopher who proposes a list of basic goods. The use to which he puts the list is different: I'm discussing what it is to live a good life, and he proposes a comprehensive account of our moral obligations. Nevertheless, what he says about choice has some relevance.

First, some background. Life, knowledge, play, aesthetic experience, friendship, practical reasonableness, and religion, make it onto Finnis's list. He thinks it's a matter of basic reason to see the fundamental value of these things. Their goodness is, in some sense, written into the universe. Why is knowledge good? It just is, and if you'll just use your God-given reason (yes, Finnis puts it this way), you'll see that it's good. The morally right thing to do is always what promotes these various good things. There's the added stipulation that a moral person attaches equal importance to the good of every individual, and equal importance to every kind of good:

> The commitments must be stable and harmonious. They must give some place to each of the basic aspects of human well-being . . . No good should be accorded overriding, unconditional, exclusive significance. Each must be pursued creatively and with constancy. No choice may involve the direct suppression of any basic aspect of the well-being of any person.

The tricky thing is how to proceed when the fundamental goods come into conflict. Finnis's book is a bit short on examples, but here's an interesting one, using his list of goods. You are a high school principal. One of your students is a Muslim girl from a very conservative family. She has embraced the religious beliefs of her family, and thinks she must veil herself head to toe. In such clothing, she cannot fully participate in her P.E. class. Don't think of this in the framework of the American or the French or any other legal system; don't imagine the ACLU or Amnesty International is watching the case closely. Your only concern is to do what is right, not to stay within existing law. What are you to do?

The girl's religion must be respected, and the value of play must be acknowledged; neither must be given "overriding, unconditional, exclusive significance." One option might be to segregate boys and girls, so that the girl can remove her *abaya* and participate fully (that's how some schools in Islamic countries handle the problem). But that's not practically feasible. You could require the girl to get equivalent exercise on her own time. Sure, but if all else fails, and you have to choose between play and religion – she removes the *abaya* and plays soccer, or she keeps it on and sits on the sidelines – how are you to choose? Finnis says all you can do is regard the values equitably and . . . just choose.

The "just choose" approach pops up in the most dissimilar philosopher I can imagine, the mid-twentieth-century French existentialist Jean-Paul Sartre. Finnis is a Catholic steeped in the natural law tradition of Aristotle and Aquinas. The basic values, for him, are real and objective and discernible by reason. Sartre forswears all these venerable notions, but arrives at a not dissimilar conclusion about choice. His famous example, in the 1948 classic "Existentialism is a Humanism," concerns a young man who is wrestling with a critical choice during World War II. Should he join the resistance or stay home to take care of his ailing and frightened mother? The young man looks for advice from ethical theories, from his priest, and finally from Sartre. And Sartre tells him there is no objective answer. "Just invent," he says.

Both Finnis and Sartre are minimalists about ultimate choices, the choices we make between things that are fundamentally good, but good in different ways. Transposing into the present key, the issue is how Penelope (for example) should choose between the growth that school offers and the autonomy that quitting would restore. Finnis might counsel adopting an equitable attitude toward the values at stake, which is not much to go by, and Sartre would say even less: "Invent!"

On the face of it, there is much more to making choices. These philosophers are leaving out both rational/calculative aspects of choice and emotional elements. To return to Penelope's choice between getting a college degree and staying home: her reflections will inevitably involve more than the bare recognition of autonomy and growth as good things. A particular morsel of autonomy can be more or less good than a particular morsel of growth. Penelope wouldn't choose to attend a severely regimented class that took away vast amounts of autonomy, if she thought the growth to be gained was minute. The good lost would be far too great, in comparison to the good gained. If we reason this way – and surely we often do – Finnis thinks we're making a mistake. We can't actually make comparative judgments, especially when we're confronted with different kinds of good.

Comparison requires measurement in the same units, Finnis insists, and we can't make such measurements when we're comparing a bit of autonomy with a bit of growth. (These are values on *my* list, but not on his.) Penelope couldn't put the autonomy and growth at stake on a "good-o-meter" and declare one to be more good than the other. A goodness scale makes no more sense than a bigness scale, used to compare a heavy rock and a large balloon. Just as the weight-bigness of the rock can't be compared to the volume-bigness of the balloon, the autonomy-goodness of dropping out can't be compared to the growth-goodness of sticking with her classes.

Finnis's argument sounds right, but the fact is that we do regularly make comparisons. If you have a grasp of autonomy as a good then you can recognize instances that are more and less significant; there are

THE WEIGHT OF THINGS

ones and tens on the good-o-meter. If you have a grasp of growth as a good, you can recognize more and less significant instances of that. In Penelope's case the good of growth or progress has to be compared to the good of autonomy. Suddenly, because the case involves two kinds of good, it's supposed to be impossible to employ the imaginary good-o-meter. But in our mind's eye, it's not impossible at all.

Still, once Finnis stings us with the puzzle of how comparisons can be made, it's hard not to scratch. Once we start to scratch, comparisons seem to require, for their intelligibility, some ultimate good that runs through all the varieties of good. It's this ultimate good – not happiness, not morality, not autonomy – that we are measuring amounts of when we compare things that are good in different ways. Some philosophers have believed in such a thing. Plato, for example, claims there is a form of The Good. Depending on how much of The Good any particular thing partakes of, it is good to one degree or another. This account postulates, unsettlingly, a mysterious substance that makes different things good to different degrees. It probably makes more sense to insist on the correctness of comparative judgments without commitment to any particular explanation for them. For Penelope, the autonomy regained might just be a bigger chunk of good – no explanation for that – than the little bit of growth she'd get from her classes (or vice versa).

Comparing the amount of good in two things is one feature of the geography of choice that Finnis leaves off the map. It's an important feature. We are constantly forced to look at the good we'd get from A and compare it to some other good we'd get from B, and then choose between A and B. This is not a befuddling task, most of the time. More good here or there? There are big chunks of good and small chunks of good, and they don't all have to be the same type of good for us to see the difference.

"How much good will come of that?" is a question we do ask ourselves before making choices. It's a relevant factor in our decisions. However, our aim is not simply to have as much good in our lives as possible. As I've argued, there are many distinct good things that are necessary ingredients in a life. This means that Penelope ought to take into account the amount of good that derives from her various options, but also the necessity of each type of good. How are these two considerations going to combine to produce one decision?

Let's assume that Penelope sees (despite Finnis's skepticism about making comparisons) that the growth-good of continuing with school is less than the autonomy-good that would be restored if she dropped out. If her aim were simply to boost the total amount of good in her life, then she would have to drop out. But there is another factor. Growth and autonomy are necessities in her life. That little bit of growth-good might be just the thing she needs. Perhaps she's been in a rut for a long time, doing much the same thing, year in and year out. She's felt stagnant, though she's always been highly independent and fully in control over her life. Because her aim is not simply maximum good, but achieving the necessities, she could reasonably decide to stay in school.

Thinking about the amount of good that comes from our options, and thinking about whether we've got enough of each necessity, are two facets of being "rational and objective" about a choice. But are we entirely rational and objective? Should we try to be? To look at this more closely, I'll turn from Penelope's quotidian problem to more dramatic dilemmas, where the role of emotion is easiest to see.

ONE OF THE BEST-KNOWN narratives of the American slave experience, *Incidents in the Life of a Slave Girl*, was written by Harriet Jacobs right before the Civil War. Jacobs was a slave who worked in the household of a North Carolina physician. Compared to plantation slaves, she lived a relatively comfortable life – as she admits. However, she suffered enormously from the master's sexual harassment. For years, she hoped to escape.

At the age of 21 she abandoned her two small children, aged five and two, and went into hiding, first with friends and then in her free grandmother's attic. Her hope was that the children's father, a local white lawyer, would be given permission to buy them. In fact, her owner's first reaction was to try to smoke her out by putting the two children in jail. They remained there for more than two months, while Jacobs continued to hide, agonizing over her situation. To come forward or not to come forward? She decided not to.

In the end the master did sell the children to their father, and (though his property) they were permitted to live with their great-grandmother. There they grew up right beneath the small, dark attic where Jacobs continued to hide – for seven years. She carved a small hole in the wall of the attic so that she could see the children playing outside, but they never knew she was there. Friends finally took huge risks to help her escape north. Amazingly, her children eventually made it north as well and were reunited with her. She provided for their education and both she and her children made a great contribution to the abolitionist cause.

Fleeing slavery eventually made Jacobs's life and her children's lives much better, but when she fled, a positive outcome couldn't have seemed likely. For a very small chance of freedom for herself and her children, she put up with extraordinary misery and let her children suffer too. For all they knew, she had simply abandoned them. You can imagine that the accommodations at the local jail were not exactly luxurious (though the children's great-aunt and -uncle were in the same cell). All of the people who helped Jacobs ran the risk of being whipped and imprisoned if their role was discovered. But of course, Jacobs imposed the greatest suffering on herself. She baked in the little crawl space in the summers, froze in the winters. She was able to sew clothes for the children and read a little, and occasionally she took breaks in a little room below, but her misery must have been extraordinary.

It could conceivably be true that she endured so much misery because the misery of slavery was even worse to her. Seven years in the attic was miserable, but it was still the happier option. It seems more plausible – indeed, obvious – that Jacobs was driven not just by a preference for less misery and more happiness, but by a strikingly intense sense of the importance of freedom and autonomy. Being deprived of so much autonomy, as a slave and a victim of sexual harassment, her hunger for freedom was huge. It was huge also in comparison to other slaves who were equally deprived. Very few women escaped slavery, because they were usually unwilling to leave their children. Most preferred to give their children the more attainable happiness of their presence and protection than to pursue remote possibilities of freedom. To them, autonomy wasn't worth the misery it would cost. Jacobs's attitude contrasts even more sharply with slaves who voluntarily went on living as slaves, despite offers of manumission. Work for a kind master could be a reasonably happy option, compared to fending for oneself and suffering the discrimination and hostility vented against free blacks in the south, and the north as well. These willing slaves may well have valued freedom and autonomy, but not with the intensity that Jacobs did. For them, it was not worth a decrease in happiness to procure it, much less prolonged, intense misery.

Harriet Jacobs wanted autonomy more than most people in the very same situation. She wanted it more, which is one thing, but she probably also wanted more of it, which is another. Some slaves presumably felt they had "enough" autonomy to the extent that they were left alone in the slave quarters, or given positions of some authority. Indeed, Jacobs had just been given a position of authority in the household of Dr. Flint's son when she escaped. For her, that much autonomy was not enough. It's not that she wanted some kind of unusually independent and self-governing way of life. She just wanted what was a matter of course for ordinary Americans of her day, who happened to be white.

The intensity with which Jacobs valued autonomy was an emotional and subjective factor in the way she made choices. Because of it, she lacked the equitable attitude that Finnis admires. Her good-o-meter was skewed toward autonomy, so that autonomy tended to weigh more, in her estimation, than happiness. Or perhaps her sense of how much autonomy is "enough" was distinctive. In any event, her state of mind was not one of cool impartiality. She fought so hard for freedom because she esteemed it so passionately.

What should we think of these subjective and emotional facets of choice? Are they to be tamed and tempered, or welcomed?

Harriet Jacobs needed a passionate love of autonomy to make it, against all odds, out of the viciously racist and violent world of the antebellum south. A more measured and equitable attitude to all of the various goods combined with a well-calibrated good-o-meter, and a modest sense of what's "enough" autonomy, could not have sustained her through those seven years in the attic. A passion for one value over others drives people to many of the activities we most admire. With impartiality, nobody would climb the highest mountains, or play the violin brilliantly. People who do these things love them out of proportion to any score they would receive on an "objective" good-o-meter. They inevitably love other things less than they really merit being loved.

The passionate elements of choice seem to be distinctively our own. The mixture of goods we prefer is one of the elements of individual identity, and having an identity of our own is a good we need in order to live lives that are overall good, as I argued in Chapter 5. Partiality means different people, making legitimate choices, won't wind up with the same distribution of all of the goods in their lives. But the idea of an ideal distribution is implausible anyway. We need both progress and autonomy, but it's fine to have a lot of progress and less autonomy, or lots of autonomy and less progress.

So is passionate partisanship just as good as, or even better than, an equitable attitude toward the various goods? Finnis is persuasive when he talks about choosing out of an impartial commitment to all the things with value, so do we really want to give up that ideal?

It's important to bear in mind the difference between Finnis's problem and mine. His question is how we make choices that affect anyone. I'm concentrating on Harriet Jacobs's choice for herself. We would surely recognize a difference between the problem the principal had a few pages back, when he had to decide what to do about the Muslim girl, and the problem the girl would have if she were allowed to resolve the problem for herself. It would not seem right for the principal to profess an ardent concern for religion, and dismiss play as a frivolity, and keep her on the sidelines. It would not seem right either for him to see play as critical, and religion as no big deal. But if the girl herself is given the problem to solve, it's another thing. Perhaps she is passionate about her religion and less so about sports, or she adores sports and has a passing interest in religion. These passions seem perfectly legitimate in her decision making, even if they are not for the principal. His main goal is to be fair, and that encompasses impartiality both to different individuals and to different values. It's not so clear that her goal should be fairness at all.

All that being said, let's take note: just as you can love another person too much for your own good, it's possible to take passion for one value too far even where decisions regarding yourself alone are concerned.

Kazuo Ishiguro's wonderful novel *The Remains of the Day* is the fictional autobiography of Stevens, an English butler. His great passion is to serve Lord Darlington with dignity and professionalism. That means doing exactly what he is told, not asking questions or taking seriously his own needs and feelings. His dedication means he ignores the romantic signals he's getting from the thoroughly delightful housekeeper, who winds up leaving service to marry another man. We sympathize deeply with Stevens, and yet we have the feeling throughout that he does not care quite enough for his own autonomy. His life seems flawed, as a result.

In Halldor Laxness's book *Independent People*, Bjartur has the opposite problem. An independent farmer struggling to hang on to his farm in early twentieth-century Iceland, he is too stubborn to accept assistance. Through a long chain of events, this winds up costing him his relationship with his beloved daughter. His life is flawed, like Stevens's is, but for the opposite reason. Bjartur loves autonomy too much. He is left miserably unhappy.

Our passions can lead to kinds of prioritizing that are surely too extreme. Caring about autonomy with no sense of proportion leaves us exposed to the possibility of having too much of it, or too little of something else. With lots of passion, we're at risk of choosing unwisely even simply for ourselves.

Furthermore, a decision about how to live my life is almost never entirely about me and nobody else. Stevens seems to be making a choice only about himself when he embraces subservience, but Lord Darlington turns out to be sympathetic with the Nazis, so that Stevens's subservience advances immoral ends. Willing to do whatever he is told, he complies when he is asked to fire the two Jewish servants in the household. Harriet Jacobs's passion for freedom was a decision about her own life, but affected everyone around her. The effect turned out to be good, but fortuitously so. The children could easily have perished in jail. The doctor could have taken revenge on Harriet by making sure they were sold out of state. Her friends could have been discovered and flogged.

Even the Muslim girl earlier in this chapter cannot think of her choice (if it's hers to make) as taking place in a vacuum. Sartre supplements his simple advice to the young man – "Invent!" – with the proviso that the choices we make have to be made in "anguish." To choose for yourself is to choose for all:

> When a man commits himself to anything, fully realizing that he is not only choosing what he will be, but is thereby at the same time a legislator deciding for the whole of mankind – in such a moment a man cannot escape from the sense of complete and profound responsibility.

In his eloquently hyperbolic way, Sartre makes a valid point. Whatever the Muslim girl does – playing soccer while veiled, removing her veil, or sitting on the sidelines – she alters, even if only a little, what it is to be a Muslim girl and she gives her classmates an education on that subject.

Where does all this leave us on passion? Without the possibility of saying anything simple. We needn't try to cleanse ourselves of inequitable passions for different values. The need to be impartial is not so clear when we are running our own lives as it when we are deciding about other people's lives. Our passions make us who we are, and can't be said to put us off course relative to some ideal distribution of goods. There isn't one. On the other hand, we'd be wrong to give passion free reign. Our decisions for ourselves make a difference to others. And even apart from that, they can drive us in the direction of seriously flawed lives.

GOOD CHOOSING INCLUDES RATIONAL and calculative elements and also passionate elements. It calls for a kind of intelligence – being able to weigh the good in different things and recognize the essential role of different types of good. But it also allows for emotional intensity. We can recognize some people as good choosers – those who combine these intelligent and passionate elements well – and people who are not so good, who don't have the zeal that passion provides, or have too much zeal for one thing.

Fortunately, most of us aren't faced with choices as painful as the one Harriet Jacobs had to make. Occasionally we encounter a really difficult decision, but Penelope's dilemma about going to school is the stuff of everyday life. To make such a decision well is to recognize the important things at stake, to discount none of them, and to recognize also which are more needed at the present stage of your own life. Making this sort of choice doesn't exclude having a passion for some critical things more than others.

What should we say about a lucky person who glides toward all the good things, never having to deliberate about what's better and what's worse? Is she missing a vital life ingredient, since she never examines her life or wrestles with choices? Is good choosing itself a necessary life ingredient? It would be odd to say "no" but also odd to say "yes." If good choosing is a necessity, the lucky person who glides toward good things would be obliged to look for dilemmas in order to make her life go well. And that would be silly. Good choosing is almost always useful, because it's so rare to effortlessly come by the necessities. But a necessity? No.

Does good choosing nevertheless add something to our lives? In that case, the glider can live a good life, but the person who struggles intelligently and passionately for her good life lives a somewhat better life – unless, that is, the struggling over choices is generally painful. Nobody can fail to see the agony of Harriet Jacobs's dilemma. We all hope never to face anything so painful. But is it always miserable to work our way to the solution of a difficult problem? In Plato's early dialogues, Socrates obviously takes pleasure in debating values and alternative approaches to life. Indeed, dear reader, you might be someone who enjoys struggling with difficult decisions, since you've made it this far into this book. It might not be too self-congratulatory to say that people who have opportunities to tussle with values, and enjoy the tussle, have the potential to live especially good lives.

THE WEIGHT OF THINGS

Chapter 8

—————— Trying to be Good ——————

Morality is different. Perhaps you have a zeal for entering triathlons – or so I shall imagine. The problem is that the training time takes you away from your spouse and young children for large blocks of time. When you think about it, you realize you value your participation because triathlons are thrillingly enjoyable and because they also give you a strong sense of self. You don't want to give them up. But morally, you feel obligated to be a good spouse and parent. If you think through the problem in the way I described in the last chapter, you're going to be in trouble. For example, suppose you comfort yourself with the thought that there's "enough" morality in your life. You keep your promises, donate to charities and wouldn't dream of cheating on your spouse. Enough is enough. This is a way of thinking that seems fine when it comes to other valuable things. You might be satisfied with how happy you are and dispense with some new opportunity for enjoyment. But to say you've already got enough morality sounds all wrong. Morality is in a category by itself because, unlike the happier, or the more self-expressive, or the growth-enhancing option, the moral thing is, plain and simple, the right thing to do.

No policy would better reflect the special imperative to do the right thing than to make morality your first priority all of the time. You wouldn't need to go as far as the Stoics or Plato, and regard it as the only critical thing. Yes, other things are good, and to be pursued. But when morality conflicts with other good things, it's morality that we have to choose. It is, as we might say, the highest good, the pre-eminent good. It's the most necessary of necessary things.

What would your life be like if you made morality first priority, in every situation, throughout life? Could a life like that be good?

IF YOU GAVE FIRST priority to morality, of course you would indulge in no gratuitous cruelty, no exploiting of others for personal gain, no attacks on other people's property, no despoiling nature or beating the dog. The person who makes morality first priority will keep promises, tell the truth, be fair to friends, employees, students; he will express gratitude, take care of his aged parents. Or at least, if he ever strays from these ideals, he will do so because of unusual circumstances, and with justification. With morality as your first priority, you would give up a lot for yourself and do a lot for others. Whenever you contemplated spending money on luxuries for yourself, you would consider how the money could be better spent.

Contemporary philosopher Susan Wolf calls people who live this way "moral saints," in an article by the same name, and points out that their lives are far from ordinary. A moral saint will regard every human being's welfare with serious concern. He might even regard himself as no more important than others, and his family and friends as no more important than strangers. That degree of impartiality is required, on some moral theories: the moral perspective involves overcoming self-interest and the bonds that tie us more closely to some people than to others. On the other hand, one might regard those bonds as the basis for certain duties, so that the obligation to care for our own children is stronger than the obligation to care for a distant child. However these difficult issues are sorted out, a moral saint will certainly not take any human being's problems lightly. He will want to do as much good for all as he possibly can.

The time, place, and circumstances of a moral saint's life will determine the specific contours. Coming of age in a small village a thousand years ago, a person might run out of good things to do pretty quickly. To do as much good as possible, the villager might have to wander the world like Don Quixote, looking for more problems to solve. Today's moral saint wouldn't necessarily have to be a wanderer. Living in a much more interconnected world, we can find out where the greatest need is and respond to it financially without roaming the world. Today's saint might be able to do the maximum good by making money locally and sharing it globally. Then again, if he can teach or deliver medical care, he will go where those skills are needed.

A moral saint is going to be a hard worker. Even devoting some time to a hobby might not be allowed, except to the degree that occasional breaks are psychologically necessary. An occasional relaxing game of checkers might be OK; but a Hawaiian vacation that takes up time and money? Maybe not. What about having a family? That might not be a good idea. It seems unwise to deliberately create a diversion that will in all likelihood stop you from doing the maximum for other people. Unless a moral saint has a special reason to have children, because of a population shortage or his extremely special set of genes, he might have to avoid it.

This sounds like a caricature of the moral life. Our moral heroes mostly don't come close to being saints. Former president Jimmy Carter is a hero, to my mind, because of the work he's done around the world to promote peace and democracy and fight poverty. But Carter makes the time to write fiction and poetry and even to do carpentry. In the time it takes him to make one chair, he could no doubt do even more for the poor and for peace. Microsoft founder Bill Gates is another one of my moral heroes because of the very serious investment he's made, personally and financially, in addressing global health problems. But Gates doesn't hesitate to spend vast sums on his own amusement. He lives in a 40,000 square foot home gilded with every conceivable gadget. If he were to cut back just from insanely lavish living to lavish living, he could save hundreds more lives, or even hundreds of thousands. It's not really true that Carter or Gates make morality their first priority *all* of the time.

But there are people who come much closer to moral sainthood. Tracy Kidder's book *Mountains Beyond Mountains* is an enthralling portrait of Paul Farmer, an infectious disease specialist and medical anthropologist affiliated with Harvard University, who spends most of the year living among the poorest Haitians and running a hospital that dispenses free healthcare. He is also involved in health initiatives that benefit the extremely poor in Peru and Africa, and victims of resistant forms of TB in Russian prisons, among others. Bill Gates is one of the financial supporters of Farmer's healthcare organization, Cambridge-based Partners in Health. Gates and Farmer share a concern about the health and welfare of the very poor around the world, but the way they live their lives is completely dissimilar.

Farmer gives his Harvard paychecks directly to Partners in Health, which covers his living expenses. He lives in a tin-roofed shack in Haiti, like his patients. When he travels he wears the same clothes day after day. He is too busy helping the neediest people to spend much time in Paris with his unneedy anthropologist wife and their young child. When he is in Paris, he makes no time for seeing the sights. He does not take afternoons off to enjoy looking at art, or take nights off to go to the symphony or a movie. He does not take time off, period. Kidder writes, "He had traveled more than anyone I knew, and seen fewer of the brochure sights. He'd never been to Machu Pichu in Peru. He'd never gone to the Bolshoi in Moscow." Kidder asks Farmer to explain. The answer is straightforward. "The problem is, if I don't work this hard, someone will die who doesn't have to." He tries not to love his own daughter more than other people's kids. When Kidder asks him whether it's arrogant for anyone to think he could succeed at this much impartiality, Farmer answers: "All the great religious traditions of the world say, Love thy neighbor as thyself. My answer is, I'm sorry, I can't, but I'm gonna keep on trying, *comma*." The *comma* is part of a private language Farmer and his associates speak. According to Kidder, the word *"comma"* is implicitly followed by "you asshole." A little rough around the edges, maybe, but Farmer comes about as close as I can imagine to really being a moral saint.

VERY FEW PEOPLE ARE likely to live anything close to Paul Farmer's life. Still, his life has relevance to ours. Some of us struggle to be more like him. If we don't get very far we feel guilt and regret as a result. It's worth asking whether it's even possible to live good lives with morality as first priority. Some philosophers actually think not.

Let's first acknowledge the strongest variety of skepticism, the radical idea that practically any deference to morality is too much. Friedrich Nietzsche, the nineteenth-century philosopher, was profoundly skeptical of the moral life. Morality, with its insistence on selflessness and self-control, is a barrier to the full development of human potential, he says. At least higher sorts of people (Nietzsche is a blatant elitist) have the potential to live lives that are strong, adventurous, creative, exuberant, affirmative, and individual. Nietzsche exhorts these higher sorts to "live dangerously" and "build their cities on the sides of Vesuvius." Morality is an impediment to these people.

Nietzsche denies that suffering needs to be prevented. Suffering is a part of life, and ought to be owned and affirmed. Nietzsche practiced what he preached. He suffered terribly from migraine headaches and digestive disorders but tried to take a completely affirmative stance toward his own life. He aimed to be so positive that he could happily accept living the same life over and over again – as we would if time were cyclical and all events came back to us in an "eternal recurrence" of the same. (Sometimes he sounds as if he believes this is actually true.) Dedicating ourselves to preventing suffering is being caught up in pity, and pity is an insult to the pitied. The moral ideals that tell us to live for others and control ourselves are vestiges of living in a "herd" that has to protect itself from dangerous individuals. They are mere inventions, without any authority to tell us how to behave.

Whom does Nietzsche actually admire? Artists, intellectuals, people who "carry heroism into the search for knowledge," who will "*wage wars* for the sake of ideas and their consequences." He admires original thinkers and unconventional artists – people like himself; but also perhaps real warriors with bold and creative visions.

Paul Farmer's life makes it hard to take Nietzsche's fulminations against morality seriously. Whatever Nietzsche's willingness to tolerate migraines, it *is* important to prevent the suffering and death of poverty-stricken children. Paul Farmer actually seems to have all the Nietzschean virtues *and* the greatest possible devotion to morality. His life *is* strong, adventurous, creative, exuberant, affirmative, and individualistic. By living in poverty-stricken Haiti, and declining all the possible benefits of being a Harvard-affiliated physician, he does "live dangerously" and there's no doubt that he's built his house "on the sides of Vesuvius." It seems entirely wrong to suppose that moral saints cannot exemplify the traits that Nietzsche finds admirable. There may be some careers that preclude the full development of all the Nietzschean virtues (could you be a Nietzschean receptionist?), but helping the poor and sick isn't one of them.

A critique I can take more seriously is found in Susan Wolf's article. Wolf doesn't share Nietzsche's contempt for traditional morality or his esteem for suffering. We should take very seriously the dictates of morality, she thinks. Morality is a critical ingredient of the best life. But morality trumps *everything* else for the moral saint. That's what bothers Wolf – the moral saint's willingness to put anything and everything aside. She thinks only a person with certain kinds of flaws would yield constantly to morality.

For one, she thinks a moral saint must be lacking in passion. Why not suppose he's passionate about his good works? Well, "Morality itself does not seem to be a suitable object of passion," she writes. You can adore Russian novels, playing tennis, klezmer music . . . but morality? Since it's not a "suitable object of passion," the person who constantly prioritizes morality must simply not love other things very much.

Wolf thinks a moral saint must be incapable of the joy others feel in non-moral pursuits. If he doesn't allow himself extracurricular enjoyments, it's because his capacity to enjoy things is impaired. Since he constantly gives up other things to do more that is good, he "does not know what it *is* to truly love them. There seems, in other words, to be a kind of joy which the Loving Saint, either by nature or by practice, is incapable of experiencing." And this, she thinks, "seems to require either the lack or the denial of an identifiable, personal self."

Wolf expresses the highest regard for the likes of Paul Newman and Katharine Hepburn. The examples may mislead. It does not seem that she ought to have any problem with a Bill Gates or a Jimmy Carter. For all their commitment to good causes, they have no shortage of passion for other things. But what about the true moral saint, who doesn't allow anything to interfere with his commitment to doing good? Is this person, at least, open to Wolf's criticisms?

If Wolf were right that a moral saint's life must be lacking in passion, love, and joy, then it would be hard to imagine how the things I've deemed necessities could be present in it. Without these emotions, it does not seem as if there could be much happiness or self-expression or even much autonomy. But I think Wolf is off the mark about the psychology of people who are very, very good.

Wolf is wrong about the oddity of having a passion for morality. The fact that something is right stirs some people far more than others. There are people who feel extremely energized by being involved in a moral cause, and people who would rather be home catching up on *I Love Lucy* reruns. The passion for morality is not a love affair with some abstraction, but the intensity some feel far more than others, when morality is at stake. Just as Harriet Jacobs craved and later enjoyed autonomy with a special intensity (Chapter 7), there are people who are more ardently moral.

Tracy Kidder makes Paul Farmer's moral fervor clear, but also his love and passion for the people he helps. Kidder writes that Farmer has an uncanny ability to remember details about every individual patient. When he interacts with patients he gives them the intense personal attention that conveys to them: "You are the only person in the world who matters right now." Many of us feel this kind of love only for our own family members and friends, for the people with whom we have long-term relationships, but Farmer is different. As a researcher and a public health expert, his work sometimes takes him away from patient care, but he longs for it and feels sustained by it.

Farmer does find joy in good works, and so we do not have reason to suppose he has suppressed or extirpated his capacity for joy, or that he's a person with a self that's missing something. The joy he feels happens to be for helping his patients, not for going to art museums or playing an instrument. As for lack of individuality and blandness, nothing could be further from the truth. Farmer has a sardonic sense of humor. A Haitian patient brings him a present of milk in a dirty green bottle. He thanks the woman in Creole, and says to Kidder, in English, "Unpasteurized cow's milk in a dirty bottle. I can't wait to drink it." When a mother is angry at one son for supposedly using sorcery to kill his brother, who died of an illness, Farmer cleverly consoles her by reassuring her that sorcery wasn't involved in *this* particular case. To Kidder, he admits that he feels "eighty-six percent amused."

A person can give first priority to morality and live a wonderful life. Constant deference to what is moral won't necessarily displace all of the other things that make a life good – happiness, self-expression, and the rest. The person with the right emotional makeup can combine an extreme devotion to moral causes with all of the other goods. But can we all count on our lives being enhanced by the most scrupulous respect for moral standards? Should we regard Paul Farmer as a model and do everything in our power to live like him?

PETER SINGER COMES PRETTY close to saying so in his book *How Are We to Live?* We ought to strive for an ethical life because it's the cure for what ails us – and Singer thinks we are seriously ailing. Whether we're focused on getting rich, or being promoted, or on our own families, or on shopping or sports, we are prone to doubt and detachment: what, after all, is the point? These kinds of pastimes don't give us a robust sense of purpose. The solution is devoting ourselves to "transcendent ethical causes," enterprises that dislodge our focus from "me and mine" to everyone. Singer holds his hand out to people with empty lives and tries to pull them toward the less egocentric and more rewarding lives of social reformers, environmental activists, Peace Corps volunteers, and doctors who work in developing countries. Commitment to an ethical cause is a workable cure for emptiness, and he countenances no cure that works as well.

Paul Farmer is living proof that personal fulfillment can be found in devotion to an ethical cause. But isn't Singer overgeneralizing more than a little? What if a person is lacking Paul Farmer's emotional make up, and forces himself to take on his life anyway? Imagine the year 1000 villager once again. Suppose he loves nothing better than building huts and playing the mandolin. He's fallen in love and looks forward to surrounding himself with small children in his own hut (add more bells and whistles to the story, as your tastes dictate). What will it be like for him to take to the road, in search of more and more chances to do good? Although intellectually he might be able to get himself to see other people's problems as mattering just as much as his own, he might not have the right emotional foundation on which to build universal concern. If he tried, he'd wind up like a plain, square house trying to support a heavy golden dome.

Today's moral saint isn't inevitably an itinerant do-gooder. He doesn't inevitably have to physically uproot himself. But his attention will be uprooted again and again, as he settles into one project and continually updates his understanding of what needs to be done. He goes where he is called, avoiding or downplaying the distracting ties of love, marriage, friendship, and reproduction. If he doesn't rejoice in helping, if he cannot love the stranger like he could love a parent, wife, friend, or child, if he'd really rather be going to movies and building his own personal nest, morality is going to wind up being one of the only good things in his life. He won't be happy or self-expressive. He won't be running his own life, but rather giving control over it to a particular ideal.

This sort of a person is depicted in Nick Hornby's novel, *How to Be Good*. David is a cynical, hypercritical, self-involved, would-be novelist and author of a newspaper column called "The Angriest Man in Holloway," in which he rants and raves about minutiae. When his doctor wife has had enough of him and threatens him with divorce, he's converted overnight to very nearly the way of life that Peter Singer prescribes. He aspires to something way beyond his wife's conventional mixture of altruism and self-centeredness. He wants to give away everything that his wife and two children don't seriously need for themselves: the spare room goes to a homeless man, the kids' extra computer goes to a shelter, and even the Sunday roast is nearly given away. He wants

THE WEIGHT OF THINGS

to treat every person with identical concern, drawing no distinctions between self and other, family and stranger. The new attitude is no better for his marriage than the old one, but after a few months, he begins to relent. While he doesn't renounce his schemes, because he can't see anything wrong with them, they no longer sustain him. David is just not Paul Farmer material.

Singer's prescriptions are not a sure-fire cure for malaise; devotion to a transcendent ethical cause is satisfying for some, not for all. Shouldn't he recognize other possible solutions? The fact is that the person who is not cut out for moral sainthood sometimes has other ways to increase satisfaction. Invisible in Singer's panorama of modern society are people who are focused neither on material success nor on ethical causes. They work hard at being musicians, or writers, or historians; they devote themselves to being record-setting athletes, or climbing the highest mountains, or traveling around the world; they care for a sick parent or a disabled child; they perform a needed service – they are lawyers or doctors or accountants – but perform it in affluent neighborhoods. These activities are certainly not morally wrong, but they're not saintly either. For some people they are satisfying.

Is it just different strokes for different folks? There does seem to be some common ground between the various activities that afford deep satisfaction. The Peace Corps volunteer, who is devoted to a transcendent ethical cause, and the poet, the mountain climber, and the mother (who are not) have in common a focus beyond the self and a focus on something else that is evidently important. They all have a sense of doing something deeply worthwhile. Perhaps that's why all these people, in the midst of such different activities, feel a genuine passion.

Singer argues that people gain a particularly reliable sense of purpose from involvement in an ethical cause. The person helping others is the least likely to wake up in the middle of the night, wondering what's the point. But what's the evidence? Yes, the mountain climber can easily wonder why he puts so much energy into trying to get to the top of big hills. A mother can despair that some day her child will grow up and not need her so much. But doubts can rise up in the middle of any life. Even Paul Farmer could, if his temperament allowed him, brood about how much of a difference he's making: If I cure my patient, she'll just go on to encounter poverty, violence, and another illness . . . there are millions more that I'm not helping . . . what's the point?

For some, making morality first priority all of the time is a route to getting all of the other good things in life. For others there are more reliable routes. Even on the assumption that morality *is* one of the valuable things that go into making my own life go well, superlative, non-stop, super-charged morality is something else. It's possible to thrive in such a life, but possible not to.

WITH THIS ANSWER TO the question whether morality makes life go better (the answer is "sometimes yes, sometimes no"), the question of the priority of morality becomes more urgent. If you're more like Nick Hornby's flawed character than Paul Farmer, and every moral deed does not fill you with satisfaction, what are you to do? Give up on perfect morality, or aspire to it despite the limited personal rewards? Must we do what's morally better regardless of the benefit or cost to ourselves?

In some situations, yes. There are times when morality demands giving up one's life – literally, the whole thing. The firefighters who rushed into the World Trade Center on September 11 were doing what they had to do. The bravery of these heroes can seem to elevate their lives to the very heights of excellence. And certainly it's not always true that death ruins a person's life. When Socrates decided to drink the hemlock, it doesn't seem as if he did anything to make his life go worse. Just the opposite. But Socrates had enjoyed a very rich 70 years when he died, and his bravery at the end made him a sort of martyr for the cause of philosophy. His virtuous death enhanced his life, but the case seems like an exception. Commonly a person who gives up his life loses good years and doesn't leave much of a mark in history books or memory.

If it can be necessary to make your life go worse by risking death itself, it's got to be true that you sometimes have to put morality ahead of self-interest in less drastic ways. The right thing to do sometimes takes precedence, and what would make my own life go better is sometimes both different and secondary. There are things that I have to do, period. But many of us would like to believe morality isn't *always* mandatory. A firefighter may be in a situation where sacrifice is required, but when we're on the verge of buying a car or taking a vacation, sacrifice is not required just because somebody, somewhere, could use our help. Can we justify choosing the less moral path at least some of the time?

What we *want* to say is that morality sometimes *is* overriding – simply cannot be ignored – but sometimes is not. That mandolin-strumming fellow from the year 1000 has to refrain from murdering the village chief. Once he sees that killing him is morally wrong, he can't start contemplating doing so anyway for the sake of benefits to himself. Morality is overriding in that case. But if he doesn't want to rush off to help people a hundred miles away who are dying of starvation, that's all right. It would be better, but he doesn't have to do it. Is there any justification for such distinctions?

First gambit: It seems intuitively compelling that there are special strictures on taking action, and weaker strictures on omitting to do something. Morality strictly forbids getting up and strangling the chief. You shouldn't act that way. But if you're merely sitting around strumming the mandolin, minding your own business, morality doesn't strictly require you to get up and help the famine victims a hundred miles away. Kudos to the villager if he's willing to go and help out, but if he's got other plans for himself, that's fine. *Letting* bad things happen is not the same thing as *making* bad things happen.

There is an enormous literature on these issues, but a quick counter-example gives the flavor of the problems. If the villager saw a child drowning in a foot of water before his very eyes, it seems like he would be required to save him. Standing by idly, letting the child die, seems as bad as can be, for all the passivity that's involved. Surely a bystander should be held accountable just as much as, or practically as much as, a person who pushes the child under water.

Second gambit: Morality requires the villager to desist from killing the village chief, because he would be making the chief's death his goal. That's not an allowable goal. It's different if the villager ignores the famine 100 miles away. Helping is good, but not required, because in that case it's not as if his goal is for the victims to die. Again, there's a huge literature on this line of thinking. Critics worry that it would be odd to make so much hinge on the villager's mental purity, as if what really mattered was what thoughts entered or didn't enter his mind.

Third gambit: An intuitively compelling line separates what's the villager's responsibility and what's not. If he's standing over the chief with an axe, the chief's welfare becomes his responsibility. He ought to desist, and that preempts any thoughts about his own future. The folks 100 miles away are not his responsibility. He can go and help them, or not, as he chooses.

This last way of thinking best captures what many of us are thinking when we distinguish between what we have to do and what's beyond the call of duty, but admirable. If I have children, I'm responsible for taking care of them. There are things I have to do for them: a case where morality can't be ignored. If I made a promise, I'm responsible for keeping it (other things being equal). If I'm the grader, fair grades are my job. What I'm responsible for turns on some of my prior acts, but sometimes appears out of the blue. A child drowning right in front of me is my responsibility. If we think in these terms, we won't be able to ignore everything that goes on in far-away or less-visible places. If I am buying Nike sneakers I'd better look into the work conditions in the Chinese factory where they are manufactured. If I eat hamburger, what goes on at the slaughterhouse is my responsibility. But many of the world's problems are not my responsibility: the AIDS crisis in Africa, the earthquake on the India/Pakistan border in 2005, the endless Middle East conflict. We do have lots of reasons to be concerned with these things. I want my descendants to have a habitable world to live in; I know that I am better off in a world without destabilizing diseases and disasters. But the moral imperative is weaker. Responding to these things doesn't preempt all my other concerns. I can fit these things into the life I want to live, instead of dropping everything to do my utmost.

If we are willing to think critically about ourselves, and we're not just looking for rationalizations, can we be satisfied with the third gambit? It certainly seems true that we each have spheres of responsibility, and also true that we have special obligations with regard to things within these spheres. Nevertheless, I see many problems.

The perimeters of each person's sphere of responsibility are extremely unclear. If I am taking a walk in my neighborhood, and see a child face down in the creek, that child is my responsibility. But what if I am on a trip to Mexico and find myself besieged by poverty-stricken children? Within my sphere, or outside of it? And then, if there is an important distinction between what's inside my sphere of responsibility and what's outside of it, does it really follow that I'm not under any serious imperative to deal with problems on the outside? The fact that the interior problems are different could support a completely different stance. The primacy of the interior problems could merely mean that I ought to deal with them first, and the exterior problems second. What reason is there, really, to think of the interior problems as ones I must solve, and the exterior problems as optional? Finally, a problem with the picture is that it implies that you could insure your moral good standing by simply avoiding responsibility. If you see to it that you have no children, make no promises, buy no sneakers, then you're off the hook. There are things that it would be good for you to do, but you can take your time with them, fitting them in at your leisure.

Because of all these problems, it does not seem that we should rest content with the idea that we've given morality its due just so long as we've taken care of our responsibilities, as much as we do need to have a grip on what we're responsible for, and we do need to give those things special attention. It's good if we fulfill our responsibilities, but not obvious that once we're done, we're done. We may also need to take on more responsibilities, or respond morally to situations that are borderline, or respond morally to situations that are clearly not our responsibility. But do we need to do it constantly, unremittingly, day after day? Is the moral path always the one we're obliged to take?

THE GREAT FIGURES IN moral philosophy did not envision morality as demanding constant sacrifice, but not because their own moral ideas couldn't possibly lead in this direction. Aristotle sees virtue as every person's ultimate aim. It's not inconceivable that he could expect the good person to pack as much virtue into his life as possible, by wandering from place to place looking for new opportunities to be virtuous. But he assumes a life is lived with ties to a particular community, and with family and friends. The moral wanderer's life is outside the realm of possibility.

Kant thinks we have "perfect" duties to do or refrain from certain kinds of acts, like keeping promises and lying. We have "imperfect" duties to promote the well-being of other people, in the sense that it's up to us just when, where, and how we make our efforts. Considering that Kant sees moral worth as the only thing that's unqualifiedly good, you might expect him to propose a model of human life that's quite demanding. It is indeed demanding to the extent that the moral person will have to tolerate the possibly huge repercussions of never breaking promises and never lying. But there is nothing in Kant's writings or in his own life to suggest he envisioned the perfectly moral person as a moral crusader, always jumping on any new chance to do good for others.

Mill might seem to be most likely to have a very demanding idea of the moral life: "[T]he happiness which forms the utilitarian standard of what is right in conduct, is not the agent's own happiness, but that of all concerned. As between his own happiness and that of others, Utilitarianism requires him to be as strictly impartial as a disinterested and benevolent spectator." He defines the right action as the one that maximizes total good, for all who are affected. But Mill's expectations are not enormous. Mill defends Utilitarianism against the charge that it demands a huge amount from each person by arguing that most of us have the chance to have an impact only on a few lives; we needn't concern ourselves with the problems of society on a grand scale. Mill fails to contemplate the Don Quixote alternative: if there are no more problems locally, going on the road to find some more.

These philosophers give morality a kind of ultimate value that would make it hard to ever say there was a good reason to desist from doing more. But they wind up with rather modest expectations. That, evidently, is because of the way ideas about normal life quietly insinuate themselves into their thinking. The contours of a normal life are pre-set; they include community, family, friends, an occupation, private interests, and pastimes. Morality is something added to such a life, something that doesn't, or at least doesn't often, drastically alter its shape. There are exceptions to this, as I mentioned before – a firefighter has to rush into a burning building – but on the whole, morality doesn't require normal life to be abandoned.

Should we simply allow preconceptions about normal life to decide the question of the priority of morality in our lives, and give up on looking for justifications? Perhaps it's unrealistic and even arrogant to think our rational powers are so great that we could objectively reflect upon the very most fundamental elements of the way we live. These elements are established by a powerful coalition of forces that includes biology, culture, history, and psychology. We can't distance ourselves enough from the basic elements of life to really think about whether they are good or bad, let alone alter them.

We do need to accept some limits on our powers to objectively reflect upon and change basic patterns of life, but completely giving in to the status quo seems misguided. The status quo had to be thought about critically by people who brought an end to slavery, who questioned inequalities between the sexes, who first championed the rights of the disabled, children, and animals. We should at least try to justify our way of life – or be open to changing it if we can't.

MORALITY IS INDEED SOMETHING different from the other good things that are relevant to our welfare. No matter how much of our lives we've devoted to fulfilling the demands of morality, there are going to be more demands. The world is big and there are lots of problems to be solved. As long as there is even one person with a serious problem, there is a moral imperative to put that problem before less serious pursuits of my own. After all, I can't reasonably attach any more importance to myself than to any other person. We can put our hands over our ears, but if we "listen," moral imperatives are powerful no matter how many of them we have already fulfilled. They are something like mathematical imperatives. "Add 2 and 2 to get 4" is a command you should always follow, even if you get tired of 4 as an answer, and would really prefer 5. "Give priority to saving lives" is always good advice, even if you've already saved lots of lives, and would prefer a luxurious vacation in Maui. I believe we have the psychological ability to follow moral imperatives without any rewards, and despite high costs. But morality wears us out. As we fill more and more of our lives with good deeds, we want to turn our attention to other things. At some point, can't we at least accept our weariness, if not deny the force of the imperatives we wind up neglecting? Unless we're prepared to say that all but a few human beings have lived deeply flawed lives, we're going to have to say that there's "enough" morality in a life, long before every moral imperative has been fulfilled. It sounds funny, but the truth seems to be that you can live a good life even though you don't do everything that you really *should* do.

Can we say anything at all about when enough is enough? The argument I made in Chapter 6 was that each of the ingredients of a good life is a necessity because it corresponds to a capacity that shouldn't be wasted. If you never did what morality commands, you'd be wasting a valuable capacity. Doing what morality demands on every day but Friday won't suffice either. The capacity for morality includes a capacity to recognize important moral distinctions, and day of the week isn't one of them.

A distinction discussed above does seem to be built into the capacity for morality: the distinction between what we're responsible for and what we're not. It does not seem as if we could view a person as making good use of his capacity for morality if he could not draw a rough line around his own sphere of responsibility. If he is working for the homeless, and not taking good care of his children, or sending money to help earthquake victims in Pakistan, but not concerned about being fair to his employees, he's not making good use of his moral capacities. Those distinctions are important, and within his powers of moral reasoning.

We are impatient with a person who tires quickly where his own sphere of responsibility is concerned. If he makes a promise, the promisee is brought within his sphere of responsibility, and he needs to keep it. The fact that he made a hundred other promises, and has grown weary of keeping promises, counts as no excuse. Taking good care of children is doubtless exhausting, and we can understand a person who finds it tempting to give in to weariness, and neglect responsibilities. But understanding is not accepting.

Weariness becomes more respectable *after* we've taken care of our responsibilities. But I don't think we can settle for a picture that's black and white. The person who avoids responsibility in the first place shouldn't be satisfied with himself. By reducing the number of things he's responsible for, he winds up squandering his potential for morality. And even if we take on lots of responsibilities, it still doesn't seem correct for us to ignore what's on the other side of that divide. The son or daughter you dote on is no different from the distant child you are more comfortable neglecting. It makes sense to feel obligated to feed your own child first, but not to cross the distant child off the list of what matters.

At some point, doing more and more and more will begin to reduce my own happiness, my ability to be self-expressive and autonomous. That's not true of Paul Farmer and his ilk, but I must confess that it's true in my case. Is this the point when I ought to regard my own weariness as unfortunate but acceptable? Maybe not quite yet.

The various goods that go into living a good life are not necessarily equally good. Our capacity for morality is quite possibly our most astonishing. How *do* we ever rise above personal concern and care about others, even strangers? If morality is a better thing, compared to happiness, or autonomy, or self-expression (and so on), then more morality might be worth some decreases in the other life goods. The net result of doing more that's morally right will often be an improvement to my own life.

At some point, though, the deficits in other areas will get to be "too much." It's not that I'm ever entitled to a morality vacation. No, I must still take care of my responsibilities, and be aware of what more I could do, but I can also focus attention in other directions. I can wish I were able to do more, but I needn't be completely dissatisfied with myself.

If the capacity for morality is more important to use than any other capacity, it doesn't follow that morality takes precedence in every single situation. If I have done what's immediately required, and I've taken on responsibilities, and fulfilled whatever requirements they create, and I've devoted time to what's better, I am not contemptible if I also sometimes sink into my own life, disproportionately caring about whatever happens to be vital to me and mine. I can write poetry, play the piano, take my children to the movies, invest in a non-optimal career, without feeling like an abject sinner.

But for how long? When should I get back to doing what's morally better? Which extravagances are simply absurd and deplorable? I envy the rare people who really can thrive by making morality their first priority in every single situation. The envy is not because they're having so much fun. Obviously, there is nothing easy about serving as a relief worker in a country ravaged by war or disease or a natural disaster. But people like Paul Farmer not only do enormous good for others, and enjoy the satisfaction of doing so, but they are also spared a certain amount of mental turmoil.

Just what to choose in a specific situation is not easy to say. Let's return to the problems of the triathlete at the beginning of the chapter – a person we were pretending to be you. You can see that, morally speaking, it would be best if you spent more time with your children. Clearly, they are your responsibility. Are you really required to stop competing, or is it just better? If it's just better, will you be wasting your capacity for morality if you don't do it? To make up for the waste, is it good enough to donate to a good cause? Or do you have to compensate by doing good things for your kids? What should you do?

Abandoning the simple formula that morality trumps everything else lands us on unfirm ground. As hard as it is to be Paul Farmer, there is one difficult task that moral saints are spared: deciding when morality has to be heeded. The ideas I've put forth here provide only the broadest of guidelines; they don't resolve many dilemmas. But perhaps that's as it should be. We do struggle over how good we need to be. It would come as a huge surprise if any neat and simple principle could bring those struggles to an end.

Chapter 9

——— The Religious Realm ———

Tolstoy grew dissatisfied at the midpoint of his life because everything – his books, his family, his very self – seemed to be destined for the same end: decay and then death. The thought that everything is transient was unbearable to him. His crisis drew him to seek religious faith, and once he had it, he began to focus his life on lasting things – union with God both in this life and in the next, and obeying God's commands, especially as expressed in the Sermon on the Mount.

Transcending finitude and death, uniting with a supreme being, surviving in an afterlife – these are good things, surely, and they are the sort of good things that would make a life better. But are they necessary? Would your life be seriously flawed if you couldn't have them? That was Tolstoy's view. Furthermore, he thought this particular necessity ought to be his highest priority, the predominant focus of his energies. He credited his new religious devotion with giving him a sustaining sense of purpose for the rest of his life.

If Tolstoy was right, then the picture of the good life I've been painting is seriously incomplete; in fact it's like a still life with nothing but a background. Transcendence needs to be set into the picture now, and placed in the foreground. The critical question, of course, is whether he *was* right.

In Chapter 6, I argued that some ingredients must be present in any conceivable life that is good. Happiness is an example. A creature without consciousness, or whose conscious experience is relentlessly miserable, cannot even conceivably be living a good life. Other necessities are rooted in abilities. When there's a capacity for some broad and fundamental form of good, achieving some measure of that good is a necessity:

wasting the capacity creates a flaw that can't be overcome by extra help-
ings of other good things. If transcendence is a necessity, then it's either
an absolute necessity (no conceivable good life without it) or a relative
necessity that's rooted in our capacities (it's both possible for us to achieve
and too good to waste).

Tolstoy thought of transcendence as an absolute necessity. Before his
conversion, he didn't believe in God or an afterlife, and therefore couldn't
have thought anyone had the capacity to actually achieve transcendence.
For that very reason, he was convinced his life couldn't possibly be any
good: hence his misery, and his strong motivation to become a believer.
He had to believe God exists, because on that belief hinged all possibility
of thinking his life was worth living.

Is transcendence really an absolute necessity? What if there is a
supreme being, but union with that being is not possible, or there's no
life after death? Some of America's founding fathers believed in a rather
remote deity, involved in creating the universe and making it run according to laws, but not so intimately involved in our affairs. Contemplating
a world like that, you might see nothing but paltry, diminished lives.
From the Platonic perspective, discussed in Chapter 1, if there's no bridge
from our lives to some more permanent realm, our lives are badly
wanting. But there's nothing inevitable about looking at things that way.
The lofty and inspiring rhetoric of Thomas Jefferson, full of the highest
esteem for human endeavors, coexisted with a spare theology. If we
woke up tomorrow morning and the headlines in the newspaper said,
"No Afterlife, No Union with God," and somehow the facts had been
incontrovertibly proven, would all reasonable people really agree with
Tolstoy that this was the worst possible news, grounds for giving up all
of our endeavors? Would we actually stop feeding our children and
sending them to school; stop going to work and enjoying books, art,
music, movies, or football games? Temporarily, many would be disori-
ented, but I think most of us would retain or eventually form a positive
image of human life.

Another way to erase transcendence from our image of the world is
to contemplate what it would be like if there were no supreme being at
all, instead of merely no bridge between the human and the divine.
Without a supreme being, could there still be good lives? It's possible to
think that there would be no good and bad at all without God; that the
very existence of value depends on divine desires or commands or perceptions, like the moon's illumination depends on the sun. If God's

existence were required to make any thing and any life good or bad, that wouldn't automatically mean anything had to be added to the list of critical life ingredients that I've been drawing up. The things on the correct list would owe their goodness to the favor they find in God's eyes, but they could still be happiness, autonomy, and the rest. At the same time, God would be necessary to make anything on the list good.

This *would* be a big concession, and I think it is more coherent to reject it than to go along with it. From the standpoint of a believer, it's easy to swallow that some things owe their goodness to God's attitudes. There are many pages of instructions in the Bible about how the tabernacle should be built. Why would a good tabernacle have exactly ten curtains, save for the fact that that's what God prefers and commands (Exodus: 26)? But when it comes to the things on my list, it's hard to seriously think that their goodness rests on divine attitudes. Happiness (for example) is good in its own right, just because of what it is; its goodness isn't anything like the moon's derivative illumination. If God wants us to be happy, surely it is because of the inherent goodness of being happy.

Let's return to what belongs on the list. Transcendence isn't a good candidate for being an absolute necessity, but what about seeing transcendence as a relative necessity rooted in our capacities? If we really can achieve union with an infinite being, and eternal life, wouldn't that be just the kind of profound capacity for good that we should not squander? Although it is far hazier what these abilities would actually amount to (compared to the ability to be happy or autonomous or self-expressive), surely if we can transcend finitude and death, we shouldn't waste the ability.

Compare two possible worlds, one deluxe, one plain. In the deluxe world, transcendence can be attained, and in the plain world it can't. In the deluxe world, some achieve transcendence, some don't; in the plain world, of course nobody does. I think there are good lives in the plain world, because transcendence is not an absolute necessity. Where transcendence is impossible, its absence doesn't mar people's lives. In the deluxe world, though, the better lives are lived by people who make use of the ability; those who squander it are seriously worse off. There are good lives in both worlds, but are the good lives with and without transcendence equally good? In Chapter 6, I acknowledged that the good in the life of an elephant could pile up higher than the good in the life of a mouse, even granting that the mouse has all the types of good that are necessary for him. By the same token, we'd have to say that the good life that does include transcendence might be a better life. If the real world is plain, that wouldn't make our lives bad, but it would mean they could have been better.

If you are unsure whether the world is plain or deluxe, it would make sense to prefer that it's deluxe, so that you could think the good life available to us is the superior type. If you're a believer, it makes sense to be glad of God's existence and glad of the possibility of transcendence. And if you believe there is no God, or no transcendence, it would make sense to think that's a pity. It's no small thing if this is "all there is," so that we have to reconcile ourselves to the possibility of untimely deaths, and can't even hope to control the future through prayer, or overcome a sense of misfortune and limitation by feeling united with everything. It would be a pity if there were no bridge from this life to another realm. But utterly heart-wrenching? Personally, I doubt there is any such bridge. I think the world is a plain world, but also plainly marvelous. Like the contented mouse, who doesn't waste time wishing he were an elephant, I'm satisfied with a life that lacks transcendence.

Before his conversion, Tolstoy's attitude about God and transcendence was much more than a preference. He thought his life was gravely marred, because he thought of transcendence as an absolute necessity. Life without transcendence is a disaster, he assumed. He contemplated suicide and lost all enjoyment of life. To want the better life that transcendence would permit is one thing; to deplore the wretchedness of life without transcendence is another. Transcendence is the good that Tolstoy found captivating, energizing, beautiful. Did he go overboard, loving transcendence too much? We'll come back to that question at the end of the chapter.

If TRANSCENDENCE IS A real possibility, then there are, conceivably, right and wrong attitudes to have and ways to behave in order to actually achieve it. At the most exclusive end of the spectrum, you might think there must be explicit espousal of specific religious beliefs, or obedience to scriptural commandments, or compliance with ecclesiastical authority, or performance of ritual, or all of the above. The only road to transcendence is through Religion with a capital "R." Specific forms of the exclusive view might see Baptism as the only road to transcendence, or Hinduism, or some specific form of Islam. In the middle of the "toler-ance" spectrum, there's a relatively inclusive view that is kinder to members of different religious denominations, but draws the line at the unbeliever: no transcendence for people who are skeptical about tran-scendence or skeptical about the existence of God.

On the most inclusive end of the spectrum, the crucial attitudes and behaviors are open to members of different religions, and to the religious and unreligious alike. They are things like feeling respect and wonder in the face of the world around us, acting lovingly and respectfully toward others, seeking to preserve what's good and fight against what's bad. If there is a supreme being, perhaps those are exactly the attitudes that he/she/it appreciates. Maybe the deity doesn't demand to be wor-shipped or even recognized. It could even be that the unreligious do achieve union with God without knowing it; that might be what we're really experiencing when, as a result of our love and respect and open-ness to the world around us, we experience a euphoric sense of awe; some people might feel that most strongly by experiencing the beauty of nature, or oneness with a crowd of people, or delight in a litter of newborn puppies, or the joy of sex.

Tolstoy was outraged by the exclusive view and a passionate cham-pion of religious tolerance, but his views are not at the most inclusive end of the spectrum. He writes: "Man is a weak and miserable creature when God's light is not burning in his soul. But when it burns (*and it only burns in souls enlightened by religion*), man becomes the most powerful creature in the world" (my italics). To embrace religion is really to embrace only very basic things – there's a God, he created the world, we can be united with him, we contain a divine "spark," we are equals because we all contain the same spark, we should do unto others as we would be done by. And he thinks members of every religious tradi-tion can and do believe essentially this (even non-theistic religions like Buddhism and Taoism). But you've got to embrace them.

I'm not worried about being sent to hell or left out of union with God or banished from the afterlife; how could I be, when I don't believe in these things? I do think, however, that exclusivism is dangerous. The most extreme form – which insists on Christian belief, or Muslim belief, or whatever it might be – has been the basis of holy wars, terrorism, missionary depredations on "heathen" societies, bigotry, and intoler-ance. Exclusivism is dangerous, and it really makes no sense. If there were very specific beliefs and rituals that God demanded of us, then many people would be out of the running, through no fault of their own. If it's Christian belief that's required, for example, then people who spend their whole lives without contact with Christians are condemned. A God like that is not, we hope, the ruler of the universe. Up to this point, Tolstoy agrees. You couldn't ask for a more vehement and eloquent ally against inter-religious intolerance. But we really do need to take tolerance a step further.

Even if it's simply belief in God that's regarded as essential, the evidence just does not convince everyone. To reason as best you can has got to be a virtue; to suspend reason and believe when it goes against the grain is not one. If it takes specific beliefs to enjoy union with God, a person who is cognitively impaired must be permanently left out. And so are young children and, of course, animals. A god who imposed any specific beliefs and practices as entry conditions would not – it seems – be a just god. If there is a deity with whom union is possible, then union with him is a necessity, but it doesn't follow that it's a necessity to go to church on Sunday mornings, or read scripture, or adopt a specific religion, or even to believe the minimum that Tolstoy sets forth. In short, what seems necessary is the union itself, *however* it's accomplished.

The holy books of the world's leading religions are suffused with the exclusionary stance. Yahweh tells the Israelites to destroy the towns of people who practice alien religions. Through the prophet Muhammad, Allah in the Koran recommends killing the infidels. In the Christian book of Revelations, there's a horrible fate foretold for those who don't follow Jesus. Modern-day denominations that are determined to adopt an inclusive standpoint certainly have a problem with the texts. It's some measure of progress toward inclusiveness to at least be epistemologically humble: the one true religion might be mine, but might be another one; we can't know for sure which one it is. That sort of humility would take much of the toxicity out of the exclusionary perspective. But it would still look at God as ultimately exclusive, accepting those who wind up in the right faith tradition, and rejecting everyone else. A more dramatic adjustment of attitude is necessary.

The liberal, inclusive view motivates the Unitarian tradition, which mixes together all the different religious traditions into one rich stew. But the liberal attitude doesn't make it impossible to cleave to one tradition, as long as you bear in mind that it isn't actually uniquely correct. It's not impossible for a Jew and a Christian (for example) to love their own traditions without seriously regarding them as superior, just as we love and admire our own children especially, without actually believing they're the best. But, if you adopt the inclusive view, you can't believe all of what any one of these religions tell us about how to find favor with God.

A religious person with a thoroughly inclusive attitude has to respect other religions, but also the rejection of religion. It's certainly tricky to maintain that attitude. You make the effort to keep kosher, or to pray five times a day, or recite the Catholic catechism, or whatever it might be. To have the inclusive attitude you have to have respect for people doing the other things, and you even have to respect someone like me, who does none of them. I think I've got some "right attitude and behavior" in the liberal sense. If there really is a deity and a possibility of transcendence – if the world is deluxe, despite what I believe – would it be fair for me to slide into the transcendence you have labored for, without so much as even believing in it? It sounds like I'd be getting something for nothing! But I'd watch out for representations of God that make him out to be the punitive president of an exclusive club.

I'VE ARGUED THAT UNION with God does belong on our list of necessities, if there really is a possibility of union with God. Supposing there is, we might even expect union with God and survival after death to dwarf all of the other good things in life, making success in this area worth a lot of failure in other areas. The amount of good transcendence adds to a life would seem to be *that* extraordinary.

What we find, surprisingly, is that our estimation of how well a life has gone does not turn disproportionately on this particular good. And that's true whether we're looking at things with a background of religious belief or of disbelief. If a person's whole life has been spent as a slave, with little autonomy and little happiness, it doesn't make the life all right after all to suppose the person enjoyed union with God and would go on to another life. We still wish she had been able to have a better life. If a person is cruel and sadistic toward others, but we suppose he finds "his Maker" at the very end, and joins God in the hereafter, we don't change our minds about the quality of his life: it was still seriously flawed. Simeon Stylites, from Chapter 2, is an example of a person whose life seems to have been flawed, even if we grant that he was successful in his primary aims – communion with God both here and in the hereafter. His days on earth were too full of pain, too lacking in worth-while activity, too morally limited, to add up to a good life.

In "The Death of Ivan Ilyich," Tolstoy's protagonist spends his final days wracked with pain and discontentment, but in the end he finds peace. He is released from psychological torment by admitting what he has continually wanted to deny. "[I]t was revealed to him that his life had not been what it ought to have been but that it was still possible to put it right." What could still be put right? His past life? No, the pivotal realization is that his life didn't go well. It's the moment of his death that's put right, and his future. He has faint glimmerings of his mother's love for him as a child, and finds love even in the room where his rather loveless family surrounds him. Finally the terror of death disappears. "'Where is it? What death?' There was no fear because there was no death either. In place of death there was light. 'So that's what it is!' he suddenly exclaimed aloud. 'What joy!'"

It's certainly puzzling why "union with the infinite" doesn't make up for all limitations and make a life overall good. After all, it seems to be *such* a good thing that no other good would be necessary, as long as it was present. Why *doesn't* it strike us that way, when it comes to examining actual (or fictional) lives?

One aspect of the answer has to do with something that's been unspoken but obvious in this chapter so far. It's just not that clear what it is to experience union with the infinite. We don't know exactly what an afterlife encompasses. Is it a real continuation of this life, with all of the possible assets this life contains? Are there opportunities for self-expression and growth and caring for others in the afterlife, or is it rather a state of intense happiness? Because we have no definite idea what transcendence really is, we have no definite idea how it compares to or combines with other things. At first glance, union with the infinite and everlasting life ought to make up for huge problems in a life. On closer inspection, they are too nebulous to factor into our thinking more strongly than other, more palpable goods.

Another reason why achieving permanence does not strike us as the predominant value in a life is that we really identify a life most especially with the 75-odd years we spend here (if we are lucky), in commerce with earthly people, places, and things. Maybe, if there is an afterlife, we will come to have a new perspective, from which the earthly stage of life will seem less important. Maybe we will look back on the first 75 years like we now look back at the days of early childhood – as somehow a time when we weren't ourselves yet. But for now, what we think of as a life is composed of a string of days and years *here*. Achieving permanence may be a necessity – I'm saying it is one, if such a thing is possible – but it may still not be extremely central to how things are going for us *here*.

Pardon the homely analogy, but think of a person who spends four years in college flunking courses, participating in no extracurricular activities, and developing no social life. We still have to say his college career didn't go well, even if it's true that all the while he was bonding with an executive who would later hire him and ensure him a superb career. Simeon Stylites may have had a relationship with and a future with God, but 30 years spent standing on a pillar didn't make his *life* a good life.

If we had a God's-eye view of our entire life span, here and in the hereafter, perhaps the weight we'd give to achieving permanence would be different, but from the only perspective we have available in this life, permanence doesn't displace or dominate everything else on the list of necessities. We need to meet our moral responsibilities, and run our own lives, and express ourselves, and all the rest, *and* (if it's possible to do so) we need to achieve union with God and everlasting life.

Is achieving permanence *really, ultimately* the most important thing, and worth the sacrifice of everything else? It doesn't even matter, unless we're sometimes forced into a choice between permanence and other things on the list of necessities. Simeon thought there were painful trade-offs. To achieve union with God, he had to give up physical happiness, and ordinary types of productivity. He had to give up being a good son (he refused to see his mother even when she was on death's doorstep). Tolstoy was something of an ascetic himself. He thought union with God meant giving up sex with his wife, and giving up wine, and giving up writing literature unless it dealt with religious themes. But these views of the trade-offs involve extreme versions of the exclusionary view of what is required for union with God: no union and no afterlife except for the select, who believe the right things, give up the right things, and focus their attention directly on God.

The inclusive view makes union with God "easier." On the inclusive view, union with God is available in the midst of writing literature, delivering babies, fighting against injustice, hiking up Everest, and so on. It's what we have when we engage joyously and respectfully with

God's creation. That makes conflicts between union and other good things more rare, and therefore makes weighing the value of permanence against the value of other things less critical.

On anything but a rather extreme version of the exclusionary view, valuing the achievement of permanence doesn't alter what's been said so far in this book. All the things I've discussed are still critical ingredients of a good life; transcendence has to be added to the list if it's possible, but it doesn't displace or overshadow the other ingredients.

You are in fact an atheist or an agnostic – at least so I'll now suppose. It could be you're wrong about God, and it could be that you're experiencing union with him and heading for an afterlife despite your beliefs. But suppose you're not wrong, that you really do live in a world without a supreme being. Is permanence outside the realm of possibility?

Well, not altogether. You can still focus your energies on relatively permanent things. You could seek knowledge of the enduring aspects of reality: become a physicist rather than a political pollster or market researcher. If there's no real possibility of immortality, you could still strive for quasi-immortality by trying to leave an enduring mark on the world. Participating in a religious tradition can be a way of overcoming transience, entirely apart from any divine realities. That's part of the reason why, in spite of a naturalistic view of things, my own Jewish identity is important to me. I enjoy the thought that a long chain links me to a distinct people in the remote past and the future.

Tolstoy seems to have felt no attraction for semi-permanence. He had it in abundance. His books dealt with perennial human issues, and not fads. And he knew they were going to endure. He had so many children that he was assured of descendants for a very long time. Quasi-immortality didn't interest him, but I think it does interest many people. Even those who don't think this is a godless world often attach importance to living on, in some sense, in this world. As much as they are pleased with the idea of a life that continues elsewhere, they are displeased with the idea of a life that doesn't continue here.

Not just any continuation will do. We want the *good* life we have lived to continue, and that means the marks we leave have to reflect that goodness. It gives us no comfort to know the graffiti we etched into a tree, in a moment of immaturity, will be there after our deaths. We don't want a transgression to live on in people's memories. There's not a great deal of comfort in the thought that an irredeemably wicked child of ours is going to be around for years after we've died. We want to live on in the positive marks we've left behind. We want to have an enduring *positive* impact.

We care about all this, but how much? Obviously, it varies from person to person. It also varies from epoch to epoch. As they contemplate mortal combat, Homeric heroes proclaim that they prefer being remembered for great deeds to the pleasures of hearth and home. Second-term American presidents sometimes start shifting gears for the sake of their "legacy."

We can measure how much we care by considering what weight we give to having an impact when other things are at stake as well. It might occur to you that you ought to have children because they'll live on after you die, but that thought is easily trumped by the consideration that, honestly, you don't like children. Then again, if you do want children, you might hesitate because you know that they'll take away time from your painting. You know that people are more likely to be talking about you in a hundred years if your art is around; and not so likely if your great-great-great-grandchild is around. These kinds of thoughts have enough cogency to them to play some role in decision making. But far weightier are the direct desires we feel to make children or not make children, to make art or not make art. Having an enduring impact has to be seen as a good – as something that can make a life better – but as a secondary good.

What of the idea that it's better to pursue knowledge of enduring things? On the whole, it does seem better, but when all things are considered, again, that thought is readily trounced by others. The pollster's knowledge may focus on something very transient, but that's not going to bother him much if he cares a lot about an upcoming election. If you adore rock music, then knowing a lot about it will be worth a lot, and it will have little significance to you that rock music is a passing phenomenon. Relative permanence has some value, but for most of us, most of the time, it is no match for the other things we value.

LET'S RETURN TO THE topic of religion. Anyone who sees religion – simply having specific sets of beliefs or doing things like saying prayers and blessings, lighting candles, going to a house of worship, or reading scriptures – as the linchpin of good living will not be very happy with the conclusions I've reached. I've said that transcendence has only possible relevance to a good life; and that religion is not the only route to transcendence (if it's something that can actually be achieved). This is a far cry from saying religion is absolutely essential. Maybe, though, I'm missing the point. Maybe religion gets its necessity in another way, and not from its connection to the good of transcendence.

Some religions are far less focused on transcendence, to begin with. A Buddhist doesn't look forward to the day when her immortal soul will be eternally united with God in an afterlife. She believes in none of the three: soul, God, or afterlife. (She does, however, hope to *transcend* the painful limitations of earthly existence and be "dissolved" and reabsorbed into the totality of being – is that at all similar?) Buddhist teaching is centrally about how we can do better and thus feel better. When I asked one of my oldest friends how she benefits from being a Buddhist, she didn't talk about any bridge to the beyond. Just back from a pilgrimage to India, where she participated in a two-week initiation rite led by the Dalai Lama, Julie talked about happiness. In an e-mail message, she wrote:

> According to the Buddha, the experience of illumination is the only true and permanent form of happiness there is. Every other type of happiness is short-lived and contaminated, and eventually turns into its opposite – suffering. Buddhism has allowed me to taste inner richness and meaning by revealing the mechanics of what is really going on in this world we think of as "real." Putting this knowledge into practice leads towards wholeness and joy and away from separation and suffering.

Religions that do focus clearly on transcendence promise other things in addition. During his crisis, Tolstoy was beset with a sense of pointlessness. Once he took on the religious beliefs of the peasants around him, the sense of pointlessness went away. It's certainly better not to have a sense of pointlessness, better in many different ways. That feeling is paralyzing: it gets in the way of attaining happiness and every other good. If having religious beliefs is critical to avoiding that feeling, then it's indispensable after all.

Let's look closely at the sense of pointlessness. Contemporary philosopher Thomas Nagel has an illuminating analysis of what causes it. There are two stances we can take toward our own lives. We can live our lives "from the inside," so to speak. From that perspective, our jobs, our families, our involvement in politics, our craft projects (or whatever!) are unquestionably important. We take what we do completely seriously. But we can also look at our lives from the outside. This is the perspective of the person (in Chapter 1) who imagines himself in the year 10,000, looking back at today; and the person looking down at the "ants" below from the top of a Ferris wheel. From the external point of view, my child is just one child in millions. It's not that important whether she turns in her homework, whether she takes a bath, or even suffers some terrible disease or disability.

From the inside, Tolstoy was fully engaged in writing his novels and taking care of a large family. But he had a tendency to adopt the external standpoint, from which he couldn't see why his books and his family mattered so much.

And now we come to cures. Religion, for many people, is an effective solution. How does the solution work? Let's take a little side-trip to the *New York Times* bestseller list. In *The Purpose Driven Life,* the mega-hit by evangelical minister Rick Warren, the argument is that a person who is strongly motivated to pursue X must believe that human life actually exists for the purpose of X. But then, that implies believing in a creator who made us for the purpose of X. They're rare, but here and there in the Bible, Warren finds a few lines that talk about human existence as having a purpose. And what is that? To glorify God. Warren claims that these religious convictions will chase away a faltering sense of meaningfulness.

Nagel says we cannot abolish either standpoint. We are engaged, committed, and serious, and at the very same time we are detached, skeptical, and depressed, or (if we are lucky) just amused by life's pointlessness – not constantly, of course, but both possibilities are ever-present. That's the absurdity of life: there's no getting away from either the commitment or the skepticism. Nagel argues that the idea that we have a ready-made purpose is really not much help. A super-smart chicken, learning that his purpose is to be eaten, wouldn't live with more resolve and forward momentum. Nagel admits, "One is supposed to behold and partake of the glory of God, for example, in a way in which chickens do not share in the glory of coq au vin." But, he says, "any such larger purpose can be put in doubt in the same way that the aims of an individual life can be. . . ." You can feel briefly indifferent to anything, even glorifying the supreme being.

Obviously, the millions of readers of *The Purpose Driven Life* find the message of the book uplifting. If you are feeling worthless or direction-less and turn to the book, you get the message that you have the power to do things that could actually glorify a supreme being. That puts a pretty amazing amount of power and worth in your hands. You (*you!*) are a jewel in the crown of a perfect being! If you believe it, it's got to be a huge boost to your morale. But is Nagel right that we can't be immunized from feeling, sometimes, that our goals – even the goal of glorifying God – might not really be worth pursuing?

It might seem that this particular goal, like no other, is self-evidently, indubitably, worth pursuing. But I think it really enjoys no such status. In fact, this particular goal is a little peculiar. If God is already perfect, why does he need me to glorify him? Glorify him in *whose* eyes? In his own? But isn't he already perfectly glorious in his own eyes?

There is another problem with trying to derive our sense of purpose from our original purpose (if we have one). A thing created for a particu-lar purpose can go beyond that purpose. Hair is for warmth, but we enjoy arranging it or even cutting it all off for the sake of style. There's nothing wrong with that, I wouldn't think. I can do lots and lots of things, such as making up stories for my children and swimming. I don't know whether these activities glorify God or not. But why should it matter? Why should I continually measure present goals I might want to pursue against the original purpose for which I was created?

I don't think Warren's version of the religious cure is likely to be effec-tive for the thinking person who is stuck in external gear. But there is another version of the religious cure with more potency, and Tolstoy made use of it.

Tolstoy's version of Christianity does not see human beings as being *for* something, like a hammer is for something. That notion is barely present in the Bible, to begin with. The creation story is not like the story of the hammer or the wheel. God simply creates human beings "and sees that it is good" (an uplifting idea, but not the same uplifting idea that is promoted in *The Purpose Driven Life*). Later in the biblical narrative, God issues many commands, proclaiming what we "shalt" and "shalt not" do. These commands played a role in overcoming Tolstoy's sense of pointlessness. Tolstoy was especially impressed with the Sermon on the Mount. Heeding these ideas about how to live, he undertook efforts to learn from the peasants on his estate and to respond to the needs of the poor. While doing these things, he was able to live his life from the inside, engaged and committed.

Tolstoy is hardly alone in finding sustenance in his understanding of what God commands. In choosing to put service to the poor ahead of every other aim in his life, Paul Farmer (Chapter 8) is inspired by the Sermon on the Mount as well. He sees himself as obeying the commands of God, and that gives him strong motivation to choose the life he has chosen. Tracy Kidder reports that most of the people working for Farmer's organization, Partners in Health, are inspired by religious faith. My friend Julie is following the teachings of Buddhism when she refrains from killing animals – even an annoying mosquito. Anyone with a sense that a certain set of commands are sacred, whether a Christian inspired by the Sermon on the Mount, or a Buddhist inspired by the Eightfold Path, or a Muslim following the words of Muhammad, has an extra source of support for his or her endeavors.

The curious thing is that religion came to be the only thing that sustained Tolstoy. He did not seem to see the intrinsic value of morality (as I believe Paul Farmer does); he could not get interested in service to the poor until religion suffused his life. After parts of the New Testament became his inspiration, he lost interest in old pleasures and talents. The Bible doesn't praise nineteenth-century novels, so he didn't want to write them anymore. Tolstoy's dependence on religion is striking, but I think we ought to see it as an exception instead of the rule. Given the arguments of this book, it would be inexplicable if religion played an absolutely critical role in human motivation. I've argued that there are many different things that are intrinsically good, and relevant to our lives; and that these things are so valuable that it would be a terrible shame to waste them. A person who fully appreciates the value of autonomy ought to be strongly motivated to achieve it, with or without religious support. Someone who looks at growth or progress as both good and necessary won't need divine sanction for efforts to grow and progress. All of the goods I've discussed are grounds for strong motivation, apart from any religious framework.

When we look at real lives, we do in fact find plenty of examples of the motivating power of these values. Harriet Jacobs was willing to move heaven and earth to obtain freedom and autonomy for herself and her children; though a religious woman, she did not think she'd been ordered by God to do these things. In fact, there are no passages in the Bible that could provide direct inspiration to escaping slaves, like there are passages to inspire service to the poor. Lance Armstrong, the cyclist, demonstrates a sense of purpose that anyone would envy. His fans are often surprised to discover, he writes, that he is an agnostic, if not an atheist. He says he races just to race, but also to prove to other cancer survivors how much they can hope to accomplish. His sense of purpose is adequately grounded in his sense of what's worth doing and in the mesh between his aims and who he is. Harriet McBryde Johnson, the lawyer I discussed in Chapter 6, is passionately devoted to opening doors for the disabled, but she's an atheist.

Religion is not critical for having a sense of purpose. Still, who could deny that the more support for our goals, the better? If one falters, others may keep you going. Recognizing what's good and necessary; doing what fits best with who you are; living a life that meshes with your own religious beliefs: these are all ways of achieving a sense of purpose. People who have them all are in a particularly good position to persevere toward their goals.

WITH ALL THE SUPPORTS there are, including religion, can we hope to occupy the internal, engaged standpoint all of the time? Might we at least say that religion provides a sort of insurance against doubt? Well, no. It seems to me that you really can always look at your life "from the outside" and find the things you're working toward less attractive than they seem from the inside. Paul Farmer is temperamentally indisposed to doubt, but one can imagine even him feeling disengaged. Though there's a perfect mesh between saving lives and who he is; *and* Farmer thinks it's inherently important to save lives; *and* he thinks he's doing God's work; all of that does not rule out an occasional undermining thought. With all that support, one can still have moments of despair. The flood of sick people is endless; I can help only a few. Why work so hard to save lives, when living things die everyday? Once a person's dead, she's free of suffering anyway . . .

Before we become too concerned, we ought to ask ourselves how much security from detachment we really want. The Stoics recommend detachment as a means of completely immunizing ourselves against misfortune – remaining tranquil no matter what. Detachment can't do that much for us, but being able to detach yourself is of some use. If you are convinced that becoming a doctor suits who you are, that it's well worth doing, and that it's good in the eyes of God, all that prepares you well for total commitment to the medical profession. It doesn't prepare you for not getting into medical school. We may *have* to change our course. And then again, we may even want to. A life is (usually) a long thing. We may be better off, in some cases, committing ourselves to one goal, losing interest in it, and then committing ourselves to another.

A bit of detachment is crucial to remaining open to reflection about what's worth doing and what isn't. We don't figure that out, and then stop thinking for the rest of our lives. The person with total confidence that his life is full of important things that are just right for him and even divinely sanctioned can become dogmatic and unreflective. An extension of this is being intolerant of the way other people live their lives. If what I'm doing is so unquestionably worth doing, why isn't everybody doing it? (Even detachment from religious views has value, according to the Buddhist monk Thich Nhat Hanh: "Do not think the knowledge you presently possess is changeless, absolute truth. Avoid being narrow-minded and bound to present views. Learn and practice nonattachment from views in order to be open to receive others' viewpoints.")

When we've wisely chosen goals (and "views"), detachment will tend to be fleeting. Often we'll settle back into the belief that our goals *are* valuable, but sometimes we'll change course. A sense of meaningfulness is fine and to be cherished. Being able to ask "What's the point?" from time to time also has its value.

ACHIEVING RELATIVE PERMANENCE BY leaving your mark does not take priority over all of the other ingredients of living well, and (more surprisingly), neither does achieving transcendence. And yet Tolstoy made union with God the consuming passion of his life, from the time of his crisis until his death, some 30 years later. After his conversion his marriage was full of ups and downs: he was an unsteady parent to his many children, and he rarely returned to the kind of writing for which he had become famous. It would take the sensitive observations of a good psychiatrist to explain exactly why he seems to have been stuck in external gear, unable to appreciate the inherent value of his activities. Is enormous success often followed by a sense of nothing left to aim for? Do successful people sometimes feel unworthy of their success, and terrified of losing it? Was Tolstoy suffering from a biological depression?

At least a part of a good diagnosis would take into account Tolstoy's tremendous passion for transcendence itself. Tolstoy's passion for the religious dimension was quite a bit like Harriet Jacobs's passion for autonomy and Paul Farmer's passion for morality. In all these cases, there is nothing measured and judicious about the way different values are weighed and pursued. One value looms large.

There is something extraordinary and impressive about these people. To love one value this strongly and single-mindedly suggests grasping its value in a way that few of us can. Still, there's such a thing as going overboard for one value, and slighting others to one's detriment, as I argued in Chapter 7. Had Tolstoy's passion actually led him to take his own life, as he often thought of doing, we'd surely say it was excessive. Had he stood on a pillar for 30 years like Simeon Stylites, we'd think he had gone overboard. But it's hard to condemn a passion that turns out well. Tolstoy wasn't exactly a joy to live with and a more balanced and equitable attitude toward different life goods would no doubt have thrilled his wife. But Tolstoy's passion led him to promote equality, charity, and pacifism, and his literary career did not come to an end.

All in all, my verdict on Tolstoy's quest for transcendence stresses the diversity of good things and of good lives. If there is no God and no possibility of true permanence – if our world is very plain – there are good lives anyway. If transcendence is possible, then achieving it ought to be added to our list of necessities. But it makes sense to think that it can be achieved in a variety of religious lives and also in non-religious lives. The other things on our list of goods aren't trivialized by this last addition. As important as transcendence must be, if it's a possibility, that aspect of life does not swallow up all of the rest. A disproportionate passion for transcendence, like Tolstoy's, is amazing and somehow beautiful, but there are other worthy passions.

Chapter 10

Taking Aim

Without happiness, autonomy, morality, progress (and so on), basic potentials are squandered and a life winds up flawed. If a person's life is going quite abysmally, then – at least in the scenarios I can imagine – more of those six or seven things will bring it up to the level of being at least good. But then what? If a person wants a life that's more than minimally good, what's next?

Presumably more of the same will make a life get even better. More happiness, more activity with moral value, more learning and progress – all of these things, as long as they're not interfering with each other – will elevate the overall goodness of your life. They are pivotal and irreplaceable, but must you continually add just these things? Are they the only life enhancers? In Chapter 5 I suggested they might not be. You can make a good house better by adding on extra rooms, beautiful flooring, chandeliers, maybe a swimming pool. Why not think of a good life as having both necessary ("A" list) and optional ("B" list) ingredients?

There are life assets that have been downplayed so far that *could* be on the "B" list. Take accomplishment, for example. You could have loads and loads of all the good things I've discussed, without being particularly accomplished. If your life is good and then you spend 10 years becoming an excellent violinist (or cook, or mechanic), that would seem to add overall goodness to your life. Balance is another thing commonly viewed as a positive. Jimmy Carter works for great humanitarian goals around the world, but he also writes poetry and fiction, and does carpentry in his spare time. He's highly educated in areas of science and government, but also a preacher. The balance he achieves is one thing we admire about him. Another plus in some lives is beauty. Being beautiful, living among beautiful things, creating beautiful things – maybe they are all valuable. Having talents and making use of them; being creative, with or without a beautiful endpoint; having a vast amount of knowledge: these and many other things seem like plusses.

How do accomplishment, balance, talent, beauty, and the like contribute to our lives? You could think that they all merely have great utility. Accomplishment opens doors, often making for greater happiness and greater autonomy. The person who becomes accomplished has a life that makes progress – one of the things I identified as a necessity. One's accomplishments contribute to a sense of identity and self-expression. But the instrumental view says there's no intrinsic value in accomplishment, balance, etc., themselves. That would put these things on the level of a good like wealth, which really is good only for what it can bring about.

At least some of the possible "B" list assets seem to have value of their own, in addition to their instrumental value. There's no black-and-white difference between these things and the assets on the "A" list. Some philosophers want to be very parsimonious about what's granted intrinsic value. If they can hold the line at one thing, granting intrinsic value to just happiness (for example), that's tolerable. Inching up to two things is nervous-making. In this book, I've recognized a large number of things with intrinsic value. There's no extra charge for admitting a few more; and the fundamental problem that's raised by seeing *anything* as good (or bad) doesn't intensify as the list grows longer. I suggest, then, that some of the things on the "B" list are also intrinsically good.

You could have qualms about this that have nothing to do with parsimony. How could accomplishment really be intrinsically good, if there are accomplished con-artists as well as accomplished artists? How could balance be intrinsically good if it's possible to balance cruelty and kindness, as well as to balance artistic and athletic pursuits? But the same kinds of qualms arise for everything on the "A" list. Someone could autonomously run his own life of crime, or make splendid progress from being a bungling criminal to being a skilled criminal. You can call autonomy and progress intrinsically good things and still admit that, while good, they can crowd out other good things, and so they can exist in bad lives. I think the same goes for the "B" list candidates. So – all things considered – little stands in the way of considering some of them intrinsically good.

Why, then, are accomplishment, balance, and the like *only* on the "B" list? The assets on the "A" list are necessities in the sense that they are such broad and fundamental goods that it's a terrible thing when they go to waste (that's what I argued in Chapter 6). The assets on the "B" list are intrinsically valuable, but have less value; they're important, but they have smaller scope. They're not at the making-fondue end of the spectrum, but they're also not like happiness or running your own life. It isn't a terrible thing if a person does lots of things reasonably well, but hasn't bothered to become really accomplished at anything. You haven't squandered a great capacity if you became a fanatical bird watcher instead of being more balanced. There's no great shame if you don't make the most of your potential beauty. So we do want to maintain, in our minds, two separate lists of things that would make our lives better.

The target we should aim for, if we want our lives to get better and better, is not like the familiar set of concentric circles. It's like a grid of different-colored squares with different hues representing necessary and optional ingredients. The necessities are different shades of green (say) and we need to aim at each one. The various shades of purple are worth aiming for too, but they're not so critical. If we start out with a life that's not going well, we need to aim at the various greens: happiness, autonomy, and the other basics. They remain central throughout our lives. But the purple squares – balance, accomplishment, and the like – are also life-enhancing.

THE METAPHOR OF AIMING at a target is Aristotle's. He assures his students that knowing the nature of the good will help them live better lives: with that knowledge, "shall we not, like archers who have a mark to aim at, be more likely to hit upon what we should? If so, we must try, in outline at least, to determine what it is . . ." His target is the conventional set of concentric circles, with virtue as the bull's eye – though he does attach some importance to other aims (children, wealth, etc.).

But now a long-overdue question. Do we really go through life constantly aiming at making our own lives good, better, best? It's a little surprising, but the answer is clearly "No." If we are like archers, our target is not endlessly our own good lives. We focus, quite rightly, on loved ones, interesting subjects, local problems, the world's problems, football, classical music, making dinner, reading books. We can aim, perfectly reasonably, at helping our children learn, preserving the habitat of endangered species, reading all of Dostoevsky, or innumerable other goals. They're all worth aiming at for their own sake. We don't aim at them merely because we think by doing so we're going to make our lives go better.

Aiming for a better life is to be expected when life is going badly, but many of us take our focus off our own lives when we feel like our lives are "good enough." Many perfectly reasonable people with good lives will not aim for even better lives, let alone some conceivable "best life." In some cases important things beyond ourselves start to take precedence. We focus on making our children's lives better, or contribute more to our communities, or to art, or to the survival of tigers, or whatever, possibly even withstanding a serious setback to our own welfare. These things do make our lives better, but when they engage us, we aren't necessarily involved with them for our own good. After achieving what we see as a good enough life, we may not care that much about graduating to an even better life, or the best life. We're happy just to coast, filling our lives with gardening or detective novels, or whatever it might be, without being concerned whether we are spending our time in the best possible way. We don't have to think of our lives as masterpieces in progress. We don't have to be crafting ourselves all of the time, as if we were going to be put on display at an exhibition.

A person who continually aimed at making his own life good, better, best would actually be in trouble. Just as Himalayan mountaineers can put themselves in peril by being too riveted on success, so can continual focus on one's own life stand in the way of actually living a better life. Most of the things that go into living a good life are hard to obtain when a person is totally focused on obtaining them. The person determined to be very happy may not sufficiently immerse himself in whatever might actually make him happy. He's too worried about being happy to focus, instead, on reading, raking the leaves, making dinner – or whatever would actually make him happy. "I really want to be somebody," repeats the directionless twenty-something, diverting her energies from whatever activities might naturally carry her toward being somebody. Many of the critical ingredients have this paradoxical character – they are incinerated by the flames of constant attention.

Focusing on one's own betterment can be counterproductive in another sense. The energy a person directed toward getting to the very best life could stop her from having concern for other people. Yes, you might be able to accumulate merit badges for taking dinners to sick neighbors, donating to charities, and visiting your aging mother, but if you're doing it all so your own life will be better, you won't actually have the character that would make your life better.

We don't spend our lives trying to reach the lofty summit of the best life. Still, what makes a life go well figures in our thoughts sometimes. We *are* sometimes like archers aiming at our own good. Besides that, when we aim beyond ourselves, what we are aiming at is sometimes the good lives of others and we still need a target. Aristotle was well aware of this dual role of studying the good life. His students were expected to gain better lives as a result of attending his lectures, but Aristotle also saw the study of the good life as a preface to political science. With an understanding of the good life in hand, Aristotle goes on in the *Politics* to discuss the way a society is to be run. Students attending his lectures on the good life (and politics) would have hoped to wind up contributing more wisely to the good running of the Athenian state.

The other-oriented benefits of understanding what makes a life go well have not been the focus of this book, but they are urgently important. It is as parents that most of us play the role of shaping the lives of others. There's no doubt that we want good lives for our children, and maybe even the best life possible. Unconsciously, we operate with some notion of what that is. We really can do better if we think explicitly about our target. If we want our children to live good lives, and we think happiness is all that counts, we will raise them one way; if we think of morality and autonomy and progress as components of a good life, there are other decisions we will make.

Teachers and curriculum designers also quite clearly operate with some notion of how lives go best. Their responsibilities are numerous: to supply a society with people who can perform necessary jobs, with citizens who can live peacefully with each other – but also to inculcate the capacity to live a good life. They really are more likely to hit the mark, if they know what they're aiming for.

The shapers of a society – leaders, legislators, and citizens themselves – are also molders of lives. Which areas of autonomy are so vital that they must be protected, and which can be compromised for the good of all? How far should government be able to intrude on the way we think, speak, love, reproduce, parent? Everyone making decisions about these things implicitly makes them with an eye to what qualifies as a decent life.

In still other contexts, some sense of what makes life go well is operative. Missionary groups are implicitly thinking about the lives of others when they try to "spread the word" in another country. Human rights campaigns will sometimes try to alter the way things are done in another country – perhaps working to give women the vote, or end the practice of female circumcision, or protect freedom of expression. Governments and non-governmental organizations invest money in specific relief operations and development projects with an eye to what counts in people's lives and what doesn't.

It's possible to have doubts about all these other-oriented applications of our own sense of what a good life amounts to. Perhaps we should restrain ourselves, doing no more than would enable others to adopt some target for themselves, and successfully aim for it. One of the theories briefly discussed and rejected in Chapter 4 comes to mind: the idea that the best life for a person is one full of whatever *she* wants, or at least would want, in a moment of thinking carefully about her own life goals, with full information. If that's correct, then our target for others ought to be minimal: it ought to be nothing more substantial than the satisfaction of their (careful, informed) desires. Isn't it dangerous to operate with a more specific and fleshed-out notion of the proper target for everybody?

It *is* dangerous. We should not judge everyone by some richly specific standard – the good life is the life of a leisured philosopher or a statesman; the good life is the life of a Christian entrepreneur with a wife and two children. The good life is my life. I think the missionary is making a mistake in thinking everyone else needs to embrace the tenets of his religion, for one example. But to avoid this kind of arrogance, we needn't retreat to the minimal desire-fulfillment standard. The target I have been characterizing in this book *is* pretty minimal. With the importance it attaches to autonomy, it recognizes that in the end people must make their own choices, according to their own conceptions of what has value. But we can endeavor to bring up our children, set up our laws and institutions, and influence affairs in other countries, so that what is autonomously chosen is not 20-inch fingernails (recall the Guinness World Record-holder from Chapter 4); not genital mutilations that inflict pain and drastically decrease pleasure; not occupations like tobacco executive; not conformity, stagnation, and mindlessness.

NEITHER WORK NOR CARING for children has made an explicit appearance yet, either on the "A" list or the "B" list. But these are the two main things that both fill and compete with each other for time, in many people's lives. They deserve some attention.

We all sense that our children are our special responsibility. If morality in general is on the "A" list, caring for your own children is a way of being moral that can't be skipped. But describing parenting in these terms doesn't do it justice. Nurturing children is deeply satisfying, in part because of the way parents have to reflect on just what kind of lives they want their children to have. Depending on myriad decisions we make about education, healthcare, home environment, what the child reads and sees, who the child plays with, what the child eats (and on and on and on), he or she winds up in a better or worse position to live a good life. As good-life engineers, we are called upon to think carefully about issues of importance on a daily basis. It takes careful thought, good judgment, and the full raft of virtues to do the job well.

Doing the job of parenting can bestow upon us all of the things I've termed necessities, and "B" list benefits as well. The happiness we get from being parents is partly the pleasure of loving and being loved. And the love we feel for our children is a special sort: it's enormous and steady and it doesn't fade. One of the things that makes parenting interesting and challenging is that the job changes as the child changes. You figured out how to manage your child's tantrums at the age of two, but now he's three, and the old tricks don't work any more. Your creative powers are called upon again and again and again. The parent grows with the child. Parenting gives us a chance to use various talents that otherwise would go to waste. Often caring for children is completely different from what we do at work, so that a life that includes caring for children is one that is more balanced. And whatever we accomplish at work, our deepest sense of accomplishment often derives from doing a good job of raising our children.

When parenting competes with work for our attention, it is a strong competitor. It is something worthy of our time and energy. But what about work? Is it a strong competitor too? Most of us simply must work to pay the bills, but if we were to stand back and ask how working makes our lives better or worse, what would we find?

It's harder to generalize. A person hard at work could be digging ditches all day and then filling them back in. Just to amuse himself, a rich crackpot could pay you to count the blades of grass on his front lawn. Nurturing children can't fail to be a good idea, while work is sometimes best avoided – if at all possible. Work can involve spending long days without any control over your own activities or even your thoughts (think of Caroline and the blue-jean workers in Chapter 5). But fortunately a lot of work is enriching (even when it's not particularly meaningful). At work we can get better and better at something and advance to new and different responsibilities. Through work we can become more accomplished, hone our talents, and balance the things we do at home with a completely different set of activities. Typically, contributing to a household's finances brings some measure of increased autonomy. In the best-case scenario, work is meaningful, creative, or even a form of moral activity, like caring for children is. Think of the work that Paul Farmer does (Chapter 8), but also the work that your own doctor does, or the work that your child's teacher does. If we're lucky, we do work that's self-defining, that allows us, over time, to come into our own. In the best cases, work has all of the "A" list benefits *and* some of the "B" list benefits.

Parenting pretty much always adds something good to a life, and sometimes work does too. It's no wonder that we can feel torn when work and family compete with each other for our time. Parenting is not something you can simply drop, but work can sometimes be reduced. What of the more drastic choice, the choice mothers sometimes make to leave work altogether?

The attention-getting books on this subject often lean in the direction of exciting universal prescriptions. Every mother should work. No mother should work. If you're a mother struggling with a work–family dilemma, and you think it through in the manner of this book, you're going to have to wrestle with it as a unique puzzle of your very own. My problem when my own children were born was not about work and family in the abstract, but *my* work – what I was actually doing then; and *my* family; and the way the different scenarios I was contemplating would affect critical variables at stake. To add to the difficulty, this kind of decision does involve the kind of anguish that Sartre discusses (see Chapter 7) – you choose what's best in your situation, but in choosing for yourself you also have some responsibility for what all women (or men) will be. And to make matters worse, there's the fact that powerful emotions bind us to our children and our work, and these emotions shouldn't be shut out of the decision-making process. As children get older and need less from parents, the puzzle changes and a solution that made sense before can stop making sense.

Looking back at the way I solved the work–family puzzle confronting me when my children were born, I can happily say I have no regrets about shifting my focus from work to family. Later on there were new puzzles and new solutions, with attention shifting back to work. Today's puzzle and tomorrow's are another matter, and naturally a work in progress.

WHO SUCCEEDS IN LIVING a life that's overall good, or even superlatively good? Not everyone, but the ideas of this book suggest that good lives are numerous and come in lots of varieties. This would seem all wrong to some of the elitists in the history of philosophy. Plato and the Stoics make virtue the sole requirement for a good life, but the virtue that can render everything else irrelevant is a rare thing that requires a very special, hyper-rational soul. You don't need any luck in externals like money, social status, and beauty to attain it, but you certainly need to be born with the right head on your shoulders. Aristotle admits the role of externals, and doesn't soften the internal requirements. So the person who has access to a good life on his view is doubly lucky. She has a mind suited to contemplation and to moral virtue, and she also has a reasonable amount of money, social status, beauty, and so on. For all the ancients, a good life is accessible to few.

Some would find even the present view too elitist. The factors that are directly relevant to living a life that's good, better, or best, are things we don't all have equally. Innumerable matters of birth and circumstance affect how happy we are, how autonomous, how much progress we make over the course of our lives, and the rest. Autonomy, for example, doesn't grow on trees. Most people around the world have their lives run for them in many ways – by employers, governments, husbands, wives, relatives, religious leaders. Living a life with an uphill shape, with growth and change leading to ever better things, means having the leisure to explore and learn. Even self-expression, which seems to emphasize the inside, doesn't happen without advantages on the outside. Things like accomplishment and beauty are granted signifi-cance (though given second priority) and they are obviously not evenly distributed.

An egalitarian impulse is a fine thing, but should be expressed in the right way: not with the fantasy that everyone actually does, right now, the world around, live the best life, but with the determination that in the future no barriers will stand in anybody's way. Certainly the bar-riers are unevenly distributed. Extreme poverty is the most obvious barrier to achieving a satisfactory life. There are cultural barriers as well. Take autonomy, for example. A country under traditional Islamic law doesn't allow people to run their own lives, in certain important respects. The women of Saudi Arabia, for example, are prevented from choosing their dress, the way they move about (no leaving the house without a male relative, no driving cars); they are limited in their ability to leave their husbands, to own property, to vote. So, if autonomy is a critical element making a life better, Saudi Arabian women are at a disadvan-tage. It may very well be true that there are more good lives in some places than others, and that some cultures foster better lives for more individuals than others do.

Don't leap to the assumption, though, that the best life is the life you're living, along with your neighbors and compatriots. We should recognize the barriers to living well within our own affluent Western societies. Our culture of money making and consumption steers us in dubious directions. Who would question someone who designs, builds, sells, or advertises cars for a living, even if the cars happen to be gas-guzzling, greenhouse-gas-emitting disasters? That person is a great success! On further reflection, it would be hard to say why this person's life isn't morally flawed, considering the harm he ultimately causes. A person living in a very traditional society may actually find himself pressed in a more worthwhile direction. There's nothing very glamorous about making shoes or tilling the fields, but these are quietly satisfying activities that serve real needs and do no damage.

A good life isn't static, but involves some sort of growth, over time. In our affluent Western culture, our sense of what growth amounts to tends to be shaped by visions of buying more, owning more, having more fun – and we have to stop and wonder whether that really is growth at all. In extremely affluent societies, we have the happiness that "stuff" brings, but the unhappiness of always wanting more and compar-ing what we have to what our neighbor has. If we need to be not just happy, but happy with the good things in our lives, that's problematic too. We are inundated by diversions. With the TV on in average households for five hours a day, who has time to enjoy anything that's really worth enjoying?

Where are the prospects really best for attaining a good life? I don't mean to argue that it really is Kabul, not Kansas. These are questions for sociologists to resolve. But a little reflection makes it clear that the list of necessities I've proposed doesn't qualify as a list of the assets affluent Westerners disproportionately possess, and everyone else lacks.

In the monty python movie *The Meaning of Life*, there's a skit that depicts a boardroom meeting where an executive says he's completed a study of the meaning of life. What's the answer? "More hats." What's funny is the idea that the question of the meaning of life has *any* complete and final answer. If the executive had a stack of ten thick volumes containing his answer, the skit would still be funny. Even if the character had said "happiness" with a straight face, or anything else more plausible, the skit wouldn't lose all of its humor. No piece of paper or book or set of books seems likely to contain the complete and precise truth about the meaning of life, or about the good life, or about the best life.

This book has certainly not exhausted the subject. I'm not fiercely attached to my list of six or seven necessities as *the* complete list, though I'd like to think I've thought about it carefully and I'm not missing lots of things or huge things. The "B" list has been drawn tentatively and without any pretense of completeness. And there are things that deserve more attention. Is love just a feeling, a type of pleasure, or is it a distinct good? Does self-respect come along with having and expressing an identity? Is it what we have when we fulfill our moral obligations to ourselves? Or is it something separate from all the other good things, and valuable in itself?

Many of the necessities I've discussed are doorways into huge subjects. If morality is a vital part of a good life, then it's imperative to know what's moral and what's not. Now we're in the field of ethics. If happiness is a necessity – what is it? A state of the brain, something immaterial? (Now we've entered into philosophy of mind.) And what should we do to obtain as much happiness as possible? Are we happiest when we're absorbed in difficult tasks, when we're relaxing with friends, when we cease desiring anything more than what we have, when we have a strong sense of purpose? Now we need to read psychology, religion, philosophy, and perhaps just sit down and talk to our friends and relatives. What are the critical forms of autonomy? Do they include the power to vote, to publicly express opinions, to drive, to choose a marriage partner, to end a pregnancy? Now we've got one foot in public debates and the other in political philosophy. What is it to have and express a self? I'd read literature to know better, as well as psychology.

After walking through all of these doors, and exploring the nature and scope of all of the necessities, we'd still have to put up with a great deal of vagueness. You can buy yourself a detailed guide for climbing a mountain. I don't think you could buy yourself a detailed guide for moving from a bad life, to a basically good life, to a better life, to the best life. What level of happiness must you achieve, before you have enough for a basically good life? A little every day, or a constantly moderate level, or a high average, over each year? How much autonomy must you achieve? Could you continue doing something that is completely meaningless to you, if you're given lots of responsibility and independence? Can ecstatic happiness get you onto the highest pinnacle, even though you're somewhat lacking in some other areas? There are no clear answers.

Those who reach the top of the mountain would have to be well endowed with everything on the "A" list, and as much of what's on the "B" list as can be fit into one life. At these Olympian heights, do you find the likes of Arnold Schwarzenegger, because he's got all the basics plus accomplishment and balance and beauty? Or do you find a person like Paul Farmer, who makes morality his first priority far more of the time than the rest of us do? Morality does, after all, have a special status among the various goods, as I argued in Chapter 8. Are Tolstoy and Harriet Jacobs up there, because it's actually best to be driven by intense, injudicious passions, or are the best lives more balanced?

At the beginning of the *Nicomachean Ethics*, Aristotle warns his students to expect the degree of precision that fits the subject. A formula is bound to be wrong, whether it says "more hats," or it specifies exactly how much happiness, what kinds of progress, what kinds of self-expression, and so on. When it comes to giving an account of how we should live, we have to be "satisfied to indicate the truth roughly and in outline." In fact, we really want no more than this. Our lives would seem far less interesting if it were really possible to approach them with an instruction manual.

So I won't be proposing any good-life king or queen. I've enjoyed spending time with all of the people in this book while writing it, from Simeon Stylites to Harriet Jacobs, Paul Farmer and Tolstoy to the Wal-Mart workers of Chapter 5. All of their lives can inspire us at least to give deeper thought to our own paths.

Notes

These notes primarily serve the purpose of crediting sources. I only occasionally make a substantive point, and it's always tangential to the main text. Flip back here at your leisure. The notes refer to books by author and title, and full publication details are given in the Bibliography.

Introduction

p. 1   Quotes from Nietzsche, *The Gay Science*, section 283. More "how to live" sections are 276, 284, 289, 290, 292, 304, 305, and 382.

p. 1   The existentialists. For example, Sartre, "Existentialism is a Humanism."

1 This Mortal World

pp. 6ff.   Tolstoy quotes. From *A Confession*, pp. 30 and 31. The extract is reprinted in Klemke, *The Meaning of Life*. Troyat's marvelous biography of Tolstoy provided the background for this chapter.

p. 8   "In the depths of his heart . . .": Tolstoy, *The Death of Ivan Ilyich and Other Stories*, p. 137. I would like to thank an anonymous reviewer for Blackwell Publishing for suggesting I bring this masterpiece into the discussion.

p. 9   Frankl quote. *Man's Search for Meaning*, p. 124. This memoir is short, readable, and unforgettable. The quote is from an essay about Frankl's approach to psychotherapy at the back of the volume.

p. 10   He said the originals were "like spring-water . . .": Troyat, *Tolstoy,*
          p. 343.

pp. 10ff. Plato's view of reality. Dialogues that express these ideas most fully
          are the *Phaedo,* the *Symposium,* and books VI and VII of the *Republic.*

p. 12   "No sensible man . . .": *Phaedo,* 114D. Socrates says this after color-
          fully embellishing his initial account of the afterlife, so he could be
          saying only that the embellishments don't merit firm conviction.

p. 12   Kindred routes. Biblical passages about the afterlife are discussed
          briefly but interestingly in the entry for "Death" in the *HarperCollins
          Bible Dictionary,* edited by Achtemeier. Pertinent Bible references are
          provided there. For discussions of the Buddhist concept of Nirvana,
          and whether it's simply non-existence, see the various articles in the
          "Nirvana" section of Smith's *Radiant Mind.*

p. 13   "Whichever way I put the question . . .": Tolstoy, *A Confession,*
          p. 53.

p. 13   "[N]o other faith . . .": Tolstoy, *What is Religion, and Of What Does its
          Essence Consist?,* in *A Confession,* p. 95.

p. 14   Life without God. Warren's case is made more philosophically in
          Craig's "The Absurdity of Life without God," in Klemke, *The Meaning
          of Life.*

2 Strange Lives

pp. 18ff. Quotes from Lecky. A brief excerpt from Lecky is in Singer's *Ethics.*
          All of my quotes are on pp. 196–7 of Singer. For this discussion of
          the desert saints, I also consulted White, *Early Christian Lives*; Ward,
          The Desert Fathers (both of which have good introductions discussing
          historical context and motivations); and Brown, *The Body and
          Society.*

p. 19   St Anthony. See *The Life of Anthony,* by Athanasius, in *Early Christian
          Lives* (White).

p. 20   The bas-relief. Go to http://www.mcq.org/syrie/aac4_gp_relief.
          htm to see an image of it.

pp. 23ff. Plato, Aristotle, Kant, God's commands. There are readings relevant
          to each in Singer's *Ethics.*

p. 25   Spinning out biases. See Plato's *Republic* throughout for the theme of
          class structure, and Book V (starting at 474d) for the argument that
          philosophers must rule. Aristotle's defense of slavery is in the *Politics,*
          Book I, Chapters 4–6. The Bible's condemnation of slavery is nowhere
          to be found. Kant's pronouncements on masturbation are in *The
          Metaphysics of Morals,* pp. 220–1.

3 Reason and Luck

p. 27   How-to-live questions. Julia Annas argues that these "whole life" questions were, for the ancients, "the entry point" for all ethical reflection. The first and last chapters of *The Morality of Happiness* draw an illuminating picture of the contrast between ancient and modern ethics.

p. 28   Athenian life. See Connolly and Dodge, *The Ancient City.*

p. 29   Aristotle on the good life. See, most centrally, *Nichomachean Ethics*, Book I, Chapters 1, 2, 7, and 8.

p. 30   Natural and unforced. The contrast between "natural" and "forced" is stressed by Williams in *Shame and Necessity*, Chapter 5 (p. 113).

p. 31   In "politics or war." *Nichomachean Ethics*, Book X, Chapter 7, at 1177b5–15. Aristotle's praise for the philosopher's life is in Book X, Chapters 7–8. All of the Aristotle quotes in this chapter are from the Irwin translation.

p. 32   Aristotle on virtue (quotes). "We can be afraid . . .": Book II, Chapter 6, 1106b15. "Actions in accord with virtue . . .": Book I, Chapter 8, 1099a15.

p. 33   Aristotle on the human good (quotes). These are all from *Nichomachean Ethics*, Book I, Chapters 7–8. "And so the human good . . .": 1098a15. "Nonetheless, happiness . . .": 1099a25. "Further, deprivation of . . .": 1099b1.

p. 34   Glaucon's two lives. *Republic*, Book II, at 360e.

p. 34   "[A]ll think the happy life . . .": *Nichomachean Ethics*, Book VII, Chapter 13, 1153b15.

p. 36   The Stoics. For a general account of the Stoics, see Chapter 10 of Nussbaum's *The Therapy of Desire*. Julia Annas's book *The Morality of Happiness* was extremely useful to me here as well.

p. 37   The *Handbook* of Epictetus. See sections 1, 2, 5, 8, 14, 15, 17, 19, and 48 for the general advice. For working toward a goal: section 29; going to the baths: 4; dealing with a careless slave: 12.

p. 37   Epictetus on death (quotes). All are from the *Handbook*. "What upsets people . . .": 5. "If you are fond of a jug . . .": 3. "Someone else's child . . .": 26. "Never say about anything . . .": 11.

p. 38   "A life replete with virtue . . .": Nussbaum's *The Fragility of Goodness*, p. 340.

p. 38   Admiral Stockdale. See Stockdale's *Thoughts of a Philosophical Fighter Pilot.*

p. 39   Skin quote. *Many Paths to Nirvana*, by His Holiness the Dalai Lama, pp. 172–3.

p. 43   Aristotle on slavery. The *Politics*, Book I, Chapters 4–6.

4 Is Happiness All That Matters?

p. 46   Happiness graphs. I borrowed the idea of graphing happiness levels from Chapter 10 of Nozick's *The Examined Life*, pp. 100–1.

p. 48   The Epicureans. See Epicurus, "The Pursuit of Pleasure," in Singer, *Ethics*.

pp. 48ff. Mill and Bentham. Key excerpts from Mill and Bentham are in Singer's *Ethics* (p. 201 and p.199).

p. 49   The most significant issue for the ancients . . . Julia Annas stresses the distinctive focus of ancient ethics on "whole life" questions in *The Morality of Happiness*.

p. 51   Experience machine. "The Experience Machine," an excerpt from Nozick's *Anarchy, State, and Utopia*, is reprinted in Singer's *Ethics*. The same scenario is discussed in Chapter 10 of Nozick's *The Examined Life*.

p. 52   I regret to inform you . . . I owe the shift from future to past to Pollock, *Contemporary Theories of Knowledge*, pp. 1–4.

p. 57   William James quote. From "Good as the Satisfaction of Demands," in Singer's *Ethics*, p. 209.

p. 57   Desire-fulfillment theory. The vicissitudes of the desire-fulfillment theory are discussed by Derek Parfit in "What Makes Someone's Life Go Best?" in Singer's *Ethics*.

p. 58   Adaptive preferences. See Nussbaum's *Women and Human Development*, Chapter 2. The housework example is on p. 140, with context on p. 21.

p. 59   Rawls quote: *A Theory of Justice*, p. 359.

p. 60   Fingernail record. http://www.guinnessworldrecords.com/content_pages/record.asp?recordid=48558.

5 Necessities

p. 64   "It is like the light of a lamp . . .": Cicero, *On Moral Ends*, p. 79.

p. 64   Kant on the good will. This view is famously expressed in Kant's *Foundations of the Metaphysics of Morals*; see Singer's *Ethics*, pp. 123–9.

pp. 65ff. Caroline's story. Shipler, *The Working Poor*, pp. 50–76.

p. 66   Sewing flies. Shipler, *The Working Poor*, p. 78.

p. 67   Marriage at the age of eight. The example is from Martha Nussbaum, *Women and Human Development*, pp. 29–30.

p. 67   "a principle of each person as an end": Nussbaum, *Women and Human Development*, p. 56. The principle is discussed and defended on pp. 55–9.

p. 67	à Kempis, *The Imitation of Christ*, pp. 12, 95.
p. 68	Sobel quote. *Galileo's Daughter*, p. 82.
p. 70	Quote from Hanh, *Living Buddha, Living Christ*, p. 54. I'm grateful to a Blackwell reviewer for bringing this author to my attention, and for pointing out that my emphasis on self at least seems to clash with Buddhist values.
p. 76	Contemporary list makers. Nussbaum proposes a list of 10 capabilities that people must be able to exercise in a just society. See *Frontiers of Justice*, pp. 76–8. Finnis proposes a list of all of the basic goods, the things that morally correct decisions will promote. See "The Basic Values," in Singer's *Ethics*.
pp. 76ff.	Indentured servitude. Shipler, *The Working Poor*, Chapter 3.

6 Puzzles of Diversity

p. 83	Singer on infanticide. See *Practical Ethics*, Chapter 7, as well as Kuhse and Singer, *Should the Baby Live?*
p. 85	Mr. Spock. Thanks to an anonymous Blackwell reviewer for suggesting Spock as a possible problem for the view that happiness is a necessity and mentioning the episode (I think I remember it!).
p. 86	Mill and Aristotle on being fully human. Aristotle seems to make being fully human central to the good life in *Nicomachean Ethics*, Book I, Chapter 7, but he makes attaining our highest potential, whether distinctively human or not, central in Book X, Chapter 7 (1177b30): "We ought not to follow the makers of proverbs and 'Think human, since you are human,' or 'Think mortal, since you are mortal.' Rather, as far as we can, we ought to be pro-immortal and go to all lengths to live a life in accord with our supreme element . . ." The supreme element is contemplation, which we share with the gods. Mill makes being fully human critical in some passages of *On Liberty* (p. 191), but makes achieving our highest potential critical in others (p. 193), and comes down on the side of the desire-fulfillment theory in still others (p. 197). I aligned him with the Simple Happiness View in Chapter 4, based on passages of *Utilitarianism*. Perhaps consistency really is the hobgoblin of small minds.
p. 87	Down's syndrome. My assumptions about Down's syndrome were informed by Bérubé's *Life As We Know It*, though Carlos was in no sense modeled on Bérubé's son, Jamie.
p. 87	"How can it be worth it . . .": Asimov's *Bicentennial Man*, p. 206.

p. 91   Nussbaum on disabilities. *Frontiers of Justice*, pp. 184–94.

pp. 95ff. Pigs. On their lives in factory farms, see Chapter 6 of Scully's *Dominion*. On genetically engineering pigs, see pp. 235–41.

7 Hard Choices

p. 101   Finnis quote: *Fundamentals of Ethics*, p. 91.

p. 101   The Muslim girl. Geraldine Brooks talks about female participation in sport in traditional Muslim societies in *Nine Parts of Desire*, Chapter 11.

p. 102   "Just invent": Sartre, "Existentialism is a Humanism," in Kaufmann, *Existentialism from Dostoevsky to Sartre*, p. 356.

p. 103   The form of the Good. *Republic*, Book VI, 505a–509b.

p. 105   Willing slaves. Jacobs, *Incidents*, pp. 175–7.

p. 108   "When a man commits himself...": Sartre, "Existentialism is a Humanism," in Kaufmann, p. 351.

8 Trying to be Good

p. 112   Wolf's "Moral Saints." In Singer, *Ethics*.

p. 113   Bill Gates's house. See http://www.usnews.com/usnews/tech/billgate/gates.htm.

p. 114   Farmer quotes. Kidder, *Mountains Beyond Mountains*: Machu Pichu quote: pp. 204–5; "Love thy neighbor": p. 191; the explanation for "*comma*": p. 24.

p. 114   Nietzsche quotes. *The Gay Science*, section 283.

pp. 114ff. Nietzsche's views. See *The Gay Science*. The affirmation of suffering: section 338; eternal recurrence: 341; herd morality: 116, 117.

p. 115   Whom does Nietzsche admire (quotes)? *The Gay Science*, section 283.

pp. 115ff. Wolf quotes. All are on p. 350 of "Moral Saints," in Singer, *Ethics*.

p. 117   Farmer quotes. Kidder, *Mountains Beyond Mountains*, pp. 26 and 28.

pp. 117ff. *How Are We to Live?* See Chapters 9 and 10. See also Singer's influential article "Famine, Affluence, and Morality" for his views about the extent to which meeting our moral obligations must alter the contours of our daily lives.

p. 121   The drowning child. This is a variation on an example in James Rachels's "Active and Passive Euthanasia."

p. 123   Kant on the extent of our duties. See the excerpt "The Categorical Imperative," in Singer's *Ethics*. See the Langton article in the same volume for one episode in Kant's life that suggests he was no saint.

pp. 123ff.   Mill quotes and ideas. Mill, *Utilitarianism*, p. 268. The discussion of how much the typical person has to do is on p. 270.

9   The Religious Realm

p. 129   Thomas Jefferson. In fact, he thought life could be fine with no theology at all. See his letter to Peter Carr, August 10, 1787. Jefferson encourages his nephew to inquire about God, the Bible, the divinity of Jesus, and so on, reassuring him that virtue and happiness can be his, even if he rejects them all.

p. 132   Tolstoy quote. "What is Religion and of What Does its Essence Consist?," p. 128, in *A Confession and Other Religious Writings*. Tolstoy briefly characterizes the essence of religion on pp. 118–19.

p. 133   The exclusionary stance. I'm indebted to Harris's *The End of Faith* for some of the points about religious exclusivity. See pp. 16–23. On the subject of the exclusionary viewpoint in the Koran, see pp. 118–23.

p. 135   Ivan Ilyich's deathbed (quotes). Tolstoy, *The Death of Ivan Ilyich*, pp. 160–1.

p. 136   Simeon as a son. Lecky, *History of European Morals*, vol. II, p. 130.

pp. 137ff.   Enduring marks. This discussion owes a lot to Nozick's discussion of death and traces in *Philosophical Explanations*, pp. 579–85.

p. 140   Chickens with purpose. Nagel, "The Absurd," in Klemke, *The Meaning of Life*, p. 180.

p. 144   "Do not think . . .": Hanh, *Living Buddha, Living Christ*, p. 2.

10   Taking Aim

p. 148   Aristotle quote. *Nicomachean Ethics*, Book I, Chapter 2, at 1094a20. This passage (which is also an epigraph to this book) is from the W. D. Ross/Barnes translation (in Ackrill, *A New Aristotle Reader*).

p. 149   Masterpieces in progress. I owe this point to Chapter 3 of Scanlon's *What We Owe to Each Other* (see p. 130), and to Steve Sverdlik for bringing it to my attention.

p. 151   Governments and non-governmental organizations. Nussbaum discusses the proper goals of international development in *Women and*

Human Development, making a very convincing case that the primary aim should be the fulfillment of basic human capacities, not merely increased GNP or preference satisfaction.

p. 157   Aristotle quote. *Nicomachean Ethics*, Book I, Chapter 3, at 1094b20.

Bibliography

Achtemeier, Paul (ed.), *HarperCollins Bible Dictionary* (revised edition). New York: HarperCollins, 1996.

Ackrill, J. L. (ed.), *A New Aristotle Reader*. Princeton, NJ: Princeton University Press, 1987.

Annas, Julia, *The Morality of Happiness*. Oxford: Oxford University Press, 1993.

Aristotle, *Politics* (trans. C. D. C. Reeve). Indianapolis, IN: Hackett, 1998.

Aristotle, *Nicomachean Ethics* (trans. T. Irwin). Indianapolis, IN: Hackett, 1999.

Armstrong, Karen, *The Spiral Staircase: My Climb Out of Darkness*. New York: Alfred A. Knopf, 2004.

Armstrong, Lance, *Every Second Counts*. New York: Broadway, 2003.

Asimov, Isaac, *The Bicentennial Man*. London: Granada, 1977.

Bérubé, Michael, *Life As We Know It: A Father, a Family, and an Exceptional Child*. New York: Vintage, 1998.

Brooks, Geraldine, *Nine Parts of Desire: The Hidden World of Islamic Women*. New York: Anchor, 1995.

Brown, Peter, *The Body and Society: Men, Women, and Sexual Renunciation in Early Christianity*. New York: Columbia University Press, 1988.

Callahan, Steven, *Adrift: Seventy-six Days Lost at Sea*. New York: Houghton Mifflin, 1986.

Cicero, Marcus Tullius, *On Moral Ends* (ed. J. Annas). Cambridge: Cambridge University Press, 2001.

Connolly, Peter and Hazel Dodge, *The Ancient City: Life in Classical Athens and Rome*. Oxford: Oxford University Press, 1998.

Cott, Jonathan, *On the Sea of Memory: A Journey from Forgetting to Remembering*. New York: Random House, 2005.

Descartes, René, *Meditations* (trans. D. A. Cress). Indianapolis, IN: Hackett, 1993.

Dostoevsky, Fyodor, *Crime and Punishment* (trans. C. B. Garnett). London: Penguin, 2003.

Dylan, Bob, *Chronicles*, volume I. New York: Simon and Schuster, 2004.

Ehrenreich, Barbara, *Nickel and Dimed: On (Not) Getting by in America*. New York: Henry Holt, 2002.

Epictetus, *The Handbook* (trans. N. P. White). Indianapolis, IN: Hackett, 1983.

Epicurus, "The Pursuit of Pleasure." In: Peter Singer (ed.), *Ethics*. Oxford: Oxford University Press, 1994.

Euripides, *Iphigenia at Aulis*. In: *Euripides: Ten Plays* (trans. P. Roche). New York: Signet, 1998.

Finnis, John, *Fundamentals of Ethics*. Oxford: Oxford University Press, 1983.

Finnis, John, "The Basic Values." In: Peter Singer (ed.), *Ethics*. Oxford: Oxford University Press, 1994.

Frankl, Victor, *Man's Search for Meaning*. New York: Touchstone, 1984.

Hanh, Thich Nhat, *Living Buddha, Living Christ*. New York: Riverhead, 1995.

Harris, Sam, *The End of Faith: Religion, Terror, and the Future of Reason*. New York: W. W. Norton, 2004.

His Holiness the Dalai Lama, *Many Paths to Nirvana: Reflections and Advice on Right Living* (ed. Renuka Singh). New York: Penguin Compass, 2005.

Hornby, Nick, *How to Be Good*. New York: Riverhead, 2001.

Hurston, Zora Neale, *Their Eyes were Watching God*. New York: HarperPerennial, 1990.

Ishiguro, Kazuo, *The Remains of the Day*. New York: Vintage, 1990.

Jacobs, Harriet, *Incidents in the Life of a Slave Girl*. In: Frederick Douglass and Harriet Jacobs, *Narrative of the Life of Frederic Douglass, an American Slave and Incidents in the Life of a Slave Girl*. New York: Random House, 2000.

Jefferson, Thomas, Letter to Peter Carr, August 10, 1787. http://www.stephenjaygould.org/ctrl/jefferson_carr.html

Johnson, Harriet McBryde, "Unspeakable Conversations." *New York Times Magazine*, March 9, 2003.

Johnson, Harriet McBryde, *Too Late to Die Young: Nearly True Tales from a Life*. New York: Henry Holt, 2005.

Kant, Immanuel, *Foundations of the Metaphysics of Morals* (trans. L. W. Beck). New York: Prentice Hall, 1989.

Kant, Immanuel, *The Metaphysics of Morals* (trans. M. Gregor). Cambridge: Cambridge University Press, 1998.

Kaufmann, Walter, *Existentialism from Dostoevsky to Sartre*. New York: Meridian, 1956.

à Kempis, Thomas, *The Imitation of Christ* (trans. J. Tylenda). New York: Vintage, 1998.

Kidder, Tracy, *Mountains Beyond Mountains: The Quest of Dr. Paul Farmer, a Man Who Would Cure the World*. New York: Random House, 2003.

Klemke, E. D., *The Meaning of Life* (2nd edition). Oxford: Oxford University Press, 2000.

Kramer, Peter, *Listening to Prozac*. New York: Viking: 1993.

Kuhse, Helga and Peter Singer, *Should the Baby Live?* Oxford: Oxford University Press, 1985.

Laxness, Halldor, *Independent People* (trans. M. Magnusson). New York: Vintage, 1946.

Lecky, W. E. H., *History of European Morals*, volumes I and II. London: Longmans, Green, 1898.

McCourt, Frank, *Angela's Ashes*. New York: Charles Scribner's, 1996.

Mill, John Stuart, *On Liberty*. In: Mill, *Utilitarianism and Other Writings*. New York: Meridian, 1974.

Mill, John Stuart, *Utilitarianism and Other Writings*. New York: Meridian, 1974.

Nagel, Thomas, "The Absurd." In: E. D. Klemke, *The Meaning of Life* (2nd edition). Oxford: Oxford University Press, 2000.

Nietzsche, Friedrich, *The Gay Science* (trans. W. Kaufmann). New York: Vintage, 1974.

Nozick, Robert, *Philosophical Explanations*. Cambridge, MA: Harvard University Press, 1981.

Nozick, Robert, *The Examined Life: Philosophical Examinations*. New York: Touchstone, 1989.

Nozick, Robert, "The Experience Machine." In: Peter Singer (ed.), *Ethics*. Oxford: Oxford University Press, 1994.

Nussbaum, Martha, *The Therapy of Desire*. Princeton, NJ: Princeton University Press, 1996.

Nussbaum, Martha, *Women and Human Development: The Capabilities Approach*. Cambridge: Cambridge University Press, 2000.

Nussbaum, Martha, *The Fragility of Goodness: Luck and Ethics in Greek Tragedy and Philosophy*. Cambridge: Cambridge University Press, 2001.

Nussbaum, Martha, *Frontiers of Justice: Disability, Nationality, Species Membership*. Cambridge, MA: Harvard University Press, 2006.

Plato, *Phaedo* (trans. G. M. A. Grube). Indianapolis, IN: Hackett, 1981.

Plato, *Symposium* (trans. A. Nehemas and P. Woodruff). Indianapolis, IN: Hackett, 1989.

Plato, *The Republic* (trans. G. M. A. Grube and C. D. C. Reeve). Indianapolis, IN: Hackett, 1992.

Pollock, John, *Contemporary Theories of Knowledge*. Lanham, MD: Rowman and Littlefield, 1999.

Rachels, James, "Active and Passive Euthanasia," *New England Journal of Medicine*, vol. 292, no. 2 (January 9, 1975), pp. 78–80.

Rawls, John, *A Theory of Justice* (revised edition). Cambridge, MA: Harvard University Press, 1999.

Sartre, Jean Paul, "Existentialism is a Humanism." In: Walter Kaufmann (ed.), *Existentialism from Dostoevsky to Sartre*. New York: Meridian, 1956.

Scanlon, T. M., *What We Owe to Each Other*. Cambridge, MA: Harvard University Press, 1998.

Scully, Matthew, *Dominion: The Power of Man, the Suffering of Animals, and the Call to Mercy*. New York: St. Martin's Press, 2002.

Shipler, David, *The Working Poor: Invisible in America*. New York: Alfred A. Knopf, 2004.

Singer, Peter, "Famine, Affluence, and Morality," *Philosophy and Public Affairs*, vol. 1, no. 1 (Spring 1972), pp. 229–43.

Singer, Peter, *How Are We to Live? Ethics in an Age of Self-Interest*. New York: Prometheus Books, 1993.

Singer, Peter (ed.), *Ethics*. Oxford: Oxford University Press, 1994.

Singer, Peter, *Practical Ethics* (2nd edition). Cambridge: Cambridge University Press, 1993.

Smith, Jean, *Radiant Mind: Essential Buddhist Teachings and Texts*. New York: Riverhead, 1999.

Sobel, Dava, *Galileo's Daughter: A Historical Memoir of Science, Faith and Love*. New York: Penguin, 2000.

Sophocles, *Oedipus Rex*. In: *Sophocles I* (trans. D. Grene). Chicago, IL: University of Chicago Press, 1991.

Stockdale, Admiral John, *Thoughts of a Philosophical Fighter Pilot*. Stanford, CA: Hoover Institution Press, 1995.

Styron, William, *Darkness Visible: A Memoir of Madness*. New York: Vintage, 1990.

Tanner, Michael, *Nietzsche*. Oxford: Oxford University Press, 1994.

Tolstoy, Leo, *The Death of Ivan Ilyich and Other Stories* (trans. R. Edmonds). London: Penguin, 1960.

Tolstoy, Leo, *A Confession and Other Religious Writings* (trans. J. Kentish). London: Penguin, 1987.

Troyat, Henri, *Tolstoy* (trans. N. Amphoux). Garden City, NY: Doubleday and Company, 1967.

Twain, Mark, *A Connecticut Yankee in King Arthur's Court*. New York: Bantam, 1983.

Ward, Benedicta (ed.), *The Desert Fathers: Sayings of the Early Christian Monks*. London: Penguin, 2003.

Warren, Rick, *The Purpose Driven Life: What on Earth Am I Here For?* Grand Rapids, MI: Zondervan, 2002.

White, Catherine (ed. and trans.), *Early Christian Lives*. London: Penguin, 1998.

Williams, Bernard, *Shame and Necessity.* Berkeley, CA: University of California Press, 1993.

Wolf, Susan, "Moral Saints." In: Peter Singer (ed.), *Ethics.* Oxford: Oxford University Press, 1994.

Acknowledgments

Thank you, first, to my husband, Peter Groves, for unbelievable support at every stage. He was reassuring in the early days when I kept feeling like Jack Nicholson at his typewriter in *The Shining*; brutal halfway through, whenever he thought I was straying from my goal of writing readable philosophy; and a great editor at the end, when he read the whole manuscript.

I'd also like to thank my mother, Ruth Kazez, for being supportive and involved throughout and then reading the final manuscript. Her good suggestions saved me from writing things I didn't really mean. Thank you also to my father, Emil Kazez, for reading the book and saying only nice things about it.

Thank you to my colleague Steve Sverdlik, for illuminating conversations and for commenting so helpfully on the final version of the manuscript. Several chapters are much more coherent as a result.

I have fond memories of the students who took my courses on "The Meaning of Life" at Southern Methodist University in 2001 and 2002. Class discussions about religion, the experience machine, Aristotle, Stoicism, and disabilities made a tangible difference to this book.

Thanks very much to Nick Bellorini and three generous reviewers for Blackwell. By making objections, bringing authors and examples to my attention, and commenting on my writing, they did much to improve this book.

I'd like to thank my longtime friend Julie Triolo for her careful responses to my questions about Buddhism. It was a delightful coincidence that we made e-mail contact at the moment when I needed to talk about Buddhism and she had returned from an initiation rite in India, conducted by the Dalai Lama.

And last, my daughter Becky and my son Sammy helped me write this book just by being, and then by being on my team. Thank you for two good poems, a hundred book titles, countless conversations, and a huge amount of fun.

Index